to my parents

SOUND FOR THEATRES

A Basic Manual

Graham Walne

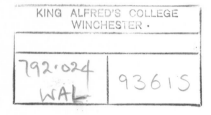
First Published 1981

Copyright © Graham Walne

ISBN 0 903931 33 8

CITY ARTS SERIES
General Editor: John Pick

John Offord (Publications) Ltd.
P.O. Box 64, Eastbourne, East Sussex.

Printed by Eastbourne Printers Ltd.

Preface

In the summer of 1979 I was pleased to receive a request from John Offord that I write a textbook on the subject of theatre sound.

The purpose of this book is to assist managers, students, technicians and performers in their work. It attempts to explain the terminology and technology of theatre sound in a single volume. It has been my particular aim to keep the language simple without shirking from explaining some of the most complex problems that can be encountered.

I have set out to provide a comprehensive work of basic reference on sound theory, acoustics, equipment and system design, with the understanding that more detailed books are available on specific subjects. In this way I hope to serve those who have to deal with theatre sound daily and yet who possess little or no knowledge of either electronics or physics, and who do not wish at this point in their lives to take a study course dealing with sound.

As the writer of this volume I must naturally take the credit (or the blame!) for what is enclosed but I would like to extend my thanks to those involved, either directly or indirectly. Thank you to all my colleagues, Fred Bentham, John Billett, Tony Bond, Owen Clark, Terry Clark, David Collison, Richard Harris, Richard Pilbrow, Francis Reid, Dorothy Tenham, Peter Woodham and John Wyckham.

Thank you also to my wife Martha for many an English lesson, to Maggie for a lot of typing, to Jill and Dick Cullyer for verification of the technical data, and to Bill Crisp for considerable assistance with the Tabs Library.

A particular thanks must go to John Offord and his staff, both past and present for their total understanding of the way in which I wanted the book to be presented.

Finally a special thanks to John Pick for allowing me to be a part of the City Arts Series.

Graham Walne
London
1981.

Acknowledgements

Rank Strand (publishers of Tabs)
Court Acoustics
Audix
Green Ginger
Trident Audio Developments
Electrosonic
Shure Electronics
AKG Acoustics
Libra Electronics
John Offord Publications
Vitavox
Ian B. Albery
Fox Waterman Photography
EDC
Sandy Brown Associates
Amcron
F. W. O. Bauch
Theatre Projects Services
Strand Sound
Solid Stage Logic

Contents

This book is written in seven individual sections. Each of these sections deals with a specific aspect of sound for theatres. It may be read as a continuous work, or used as a reference manual for those more familiar with one aspect than another . . .

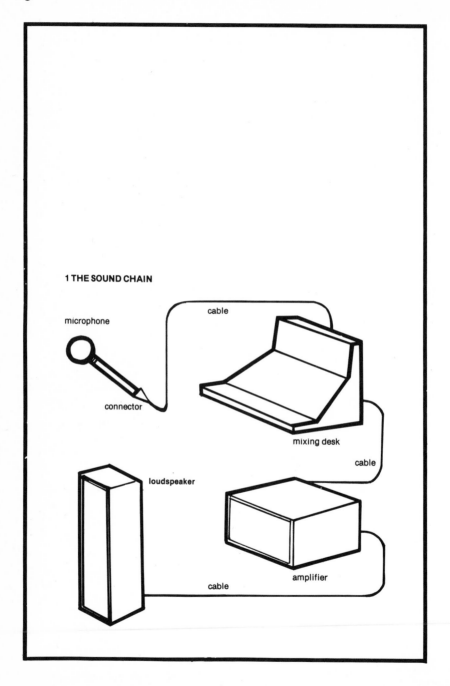

1 THE SOUND CHAIN

Introduction

This book is about a chain.

The chain of sound. And somewhere along its links you are sure to be found—performer, operator, critic, purchaser, installer or listener. But these individuals may not be linked without the equipment—microphone, mixer, amplifier and loudspeaker—not forgetting the equally vital cabling and the plugs and sockets.

From performer to listener, the chain is now complete—but as you would expect—it is only as good as its weakest link. This might be something you have little direct control over—an awkward patron hard of hearing, or an unsophisticated performer with bad microphone technique and contempt for his audience. But in between—from microphone to listener via the acoustic, there is a controllable, purchaseable system. This book is about how to make sure there are no weak links in that chain.

It is a sad fact that few people involved in the supply of a sound system know sufficient to ensure a good result. The decision-makers and purchasers rarely understand the technicalities and are prey to the subjective views of a house electrician or the rigours of the lowest tender system or both. Suppliers are rarely able to offer, of their own manufacture, a complete system to a compatible standard. Some are better at making mixers, others better at making loudspeakers. So, purchased from one manufacturer—part of the system may be of a lower standard than another. Few suppliers understand auditorium acoustics, and fewer still take them into much account when designing a system. Few acousticians like, or understand, modern sound equipment.

Given these factors, it is almost inevitable that many sound systems are of poor quality.

Sound budgets are notoriously low by comparison with other theatrical elements. Other areas tend to be awarded what they require to do a job to a defined level. Sound usually has to make do with a set figure—often what is left over when the others have had their say.

Frequently the money is unevenly spent. A good sell by the speaker manufacturer results in a poor mixer, or an attractive mixer is purchased at the expense of good microphones. The money is wasted unless all the items are compatible and of the same standard.

The good mixer cannot do its stuff if the microphones are incapable of useful pickup and the speakers are incapable of good even distribution without distortion.

We will attempt to explain the relevant parts of a sound system, and marry it to acoustics, so that the elements required of a good system may be understood.

The first section explains the basics of sound, and the language we shall meet.

Section One
An introduction to sound theory
Origins
Frequency and Wavelength
Amplitude
Sense of Direction
The Speed of Sound
Fundamentals and Harmonics
The Decibel—dB
The Ends of the Chain
The Human Voice
The Human Ear
High Sound Levels and Deafness

and to its terminology . . .

Origins

Frequency and Wavelength

When the strings of an instrument are plucked, or our vocal chords vibrated by air being exhaled from the lungs, the adjacent air particles are in collision with each other and they pass the effect of the collision down the line, like a set of dominoes falling over. The important point is that the air particles, like the dominoes, do not move from their basic position, but pass on the vibrations of the collision.

Another analogy often used is that of a stone being dropped into a pond. The ripples spread out in all directions, detectable by the wave motion—and, like sound, they decrease in strength the further away they travel from the source.

The distance from the crest of one wave to the crest of the next is called the **wavelength**, although we could measure this from any point on one wave to the same point on the next; two identical points are said to be **in phase**.

The length of waves that we hear can range from one inch to forty feet but we are not really concerned with identifying sounds in this way, unless we relate a specific length of wave to its behaviour in a room of a certain dimension. We will deal with this later in the acoustics section.

2 THE VIBRATION OF THE AIR
The particles remain more or less true to their positions but bounce into each other and pass on the vibration down the line.

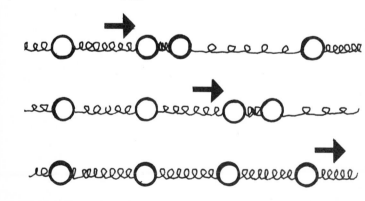

Our identification of sounds is done by counting the number of times the source makes complete vibrations in one second. These used to be termed cycles per second—cps, but are now named after a 19th century engineer, **Hertz,** abbreviated to Hz, and kHz in the case of quantities of 1000. Sounds which vibrate many times a second are known as **high frequency** and those which vibrate less are known as **low frequency.**

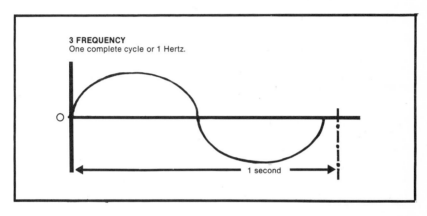

3 FREQUENCY
One complete cycle or 1 Hertz.

1 second

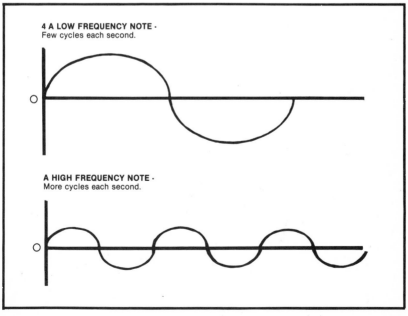

4 A LOW FREQUENCY NOTE ·
Few cycles each second.

A HIGH FREQUENCY NOTE ·
More cycles each second.

Amplitude

We have said that sound is transmitted by the vibration of air particles; the **amplitude** is the strength of the vibration.

Sense of Direction

The ear has difficulty in placing the location of low frequency (long wavelength) sounds, and is quite accurate at placing the location of high frequency (short wavelength) sounds. This is because frequencies above 1000 Hz have wavelengths shorter than the distance between the ears, so a sound above this frequency cannot reach both ears at once and at the same intensity. One ear is favoured and this provides the clue to the direction of the source. High frequency sounds are more directional than low frequency sounds.

Consider the analogy of the high frequency car horn which is concerned only with providing a warning in one direction alone, whereas a low frequency ship fog horn is more concerned with warning in all directions.

The ability of the ears to locate sources of sound in the horizontal plane is important when considering the placing of loudspeakers. Generally the ear is far less successful in locating sources of sound in vertical plane, unless it is provided with some visual clue, when the brain computes the result. Sound engineers find this valuable, as we shall see later, when positioning speakers either at the sides of the proscenium arch—or over the centre, which is acoustically often the more desirable position.

The Speed of Sound

Since sound is dependant upon vibration, it may travel through anything except a vacuum. It travels through some materials faster than others—about four times faster in water than in air, and about fourteen times as fast in iron, whilst through rubber it slows down to about one-tenth of the speed in comparison with air.

Compared to other sources, such as light which travels at 186,000 miles per second, the speed of sound is slow. It is important to note that the speed is directly related to the temperature at the time and should always be taken into account in calculations. At 14°c the speed is 1115′ (about 340m) per second and this rises or falls 2 ft per second for each degree centigrade change. The speed is virtually constant at all frequencies, although sound does travel faster in humid air than in dry air.

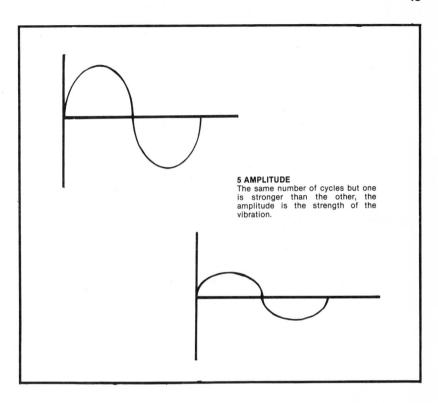

5 AMPLITUDE
The same number of cycles but one is stronger than the other, the amplitude is the strength of the vibration.

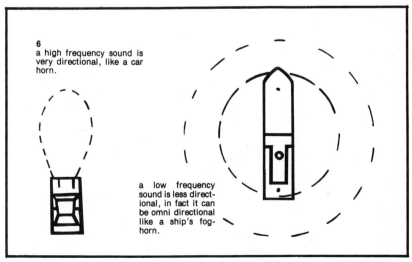

6
a high frequency sound is very directional, like a car horn.

a low frequency sound is less directional, in fact it can be omni directional like a ship's foghorn.

There is a direct relationship between the three terms discussed in previous pages, which may be expressed thus,

speed of sound = wavelength × frequency

In a large auditorium, it is possible for sound to travel so slowly over the large distances that amplified sounds reach some of the audience before the live sound. Electronic delays are used to overcome this and the calculations involve the speed of sound; we shall look at this more closely later.

As the speed of sound rises with temperature, so do the higher frequencies of many wind instruments. These cannot be tuned to overcome this, in the same way as string instruments can.

Fundamentals and Harmonics

The initial vibration of a sound source is known as the **fundamental frequency**, and the subsequent vibrations, which are exact multiples of the fundamental frequency, are called the **harmonics.**

Thus a note which has a fundamental of 100Hz will have a 2nd harmonic of 200Hz, 3rd of 300Hz and so on. The upper harmonics usually diminish in intensity, although this can depend upon how the sound source is vibrated.

It is the strength and quantity of harmonics that distinguishes the quality or **timbre** of musical instruments and makes it possible for us to identify two different instruments playing the same note.

Some wind instruments, like the flute, have few harmonics and emit fairly pure tones whereas others, like the piano, have complex sounds created by many harmonics.

Instruments also produce **overtones** which are similar in effect to harmonics, but are not exact multiples of the fundamental. The **pitch** of a note is the combination of frequencies present which identifies its position on the musical scale. It is determined by the fundamental, and dependant somewhat upon the loudness of the note.

We can use the above fundamental of 100Hz to illustrate the principle of the **octave**. This is the term used when two notes differ by a ratio of 2:1. Thus an octave separates the fundamental or first harmonic from the second harmonic, 100Hz:200Hz. At the upper end of the scale the same ratio still applies even though actual numbers are larger. Thus an octave still separates the frequencies 1000Hz and 2000Hz. Two notes separated by an octave are said to be **in tune**. The piano keyboard is a useful place to learn about octaves since each set of eight keys spans an octave, bottom A is set at 27.5Hz, A above bottom A is set at 55Hz, and so on, at 110Hz, 220Hz, 440Hz, 880Hz, 1760Hz, 3520Hz, and top A at 7040Hz.

There are specific groupings of octaves for use in noise measurement and the control of tonal content. Tables indicating these are given in the appendix.

The **transient response** of an instrument is the way it behaves when its sound source is first vibrated. For example, string instruments tend to produce notes which die away, whereas wind instruments tend to produce steady notes.

The start of this sound is called the **attack** the duration is called the **sustain**, and the final part is called the **decay**. Some instruments have a sharp attack and it is important that the sound system can cope with the virtually instant, crisp, high sound-levels often produced. Later we shall look at this more closely, since the rock industry especially is involved with transmitting a good attack with its sound.

It may be noted from the above data that any sound system which is concerned with reproducing music to high quality requires a wide frequency response to encompass the fundamentals and the harmonics. This, as we shall see later, can conflict with the requirements for a speech-only system which is better served by narrower response system.

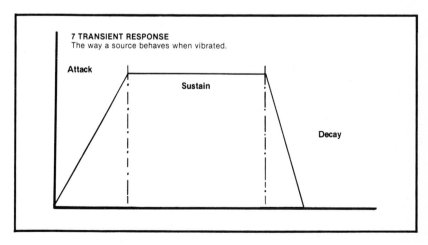

7 TRANSIENT RESPONSE
The way a source behaves when vibrated.

Attack

Sustain

Decay

The Decibel—dB

The decibel is probably the most misunderstood term in the whole sphere of sound. There are three basic points to appreciate.

Firstly, the decibel is not a unit of measurement on its own but is is a unit of comparison between two other units. Thus two other figures are always involved wherever the decibel is used.

The second point is that the decibel may be used to compare two voltages, or two currents or two sound pressure levels. Sometimes all three figures will appear, both the original currents, voltages or sound pressure levels and the decibel indication of their difference. But it is more common to find the decibel figure appearing on its own.

When this happens, it means that one of the two original measurements was an agreed international reference point. Hence the decibel shows the difference between the other original measurement and the international reference point. In all cases the reference point is known as zero level, or OdB. We will meet this term most with respect to sound pressure level, because this is the way we measure the level of sound in an auditorium. Zero level of sound pressure (know as SPL) is defined as the smallest sound which the ear will detect at a frequency of 1000Hz, although we should be aware that the ear is more sensitive at other frequencies.

It is also necessary to have a standard reference point for the electrical power flowing through sound equipment, so that it may be matched and appreciated when more or less power is being used. The standard is 0.001 watt. This may also be expressed as 0.775 volt across 600 ohm or OdBm, where the little m represents the milliwatt indicated above in the figure 0.001. The output of microphones is calibrated in this way as we shall see later. Once any reference point is understood, figures quoted as above that value are expressed as positive: + 20 dB etc., and figures quoted as below that value are expressed as negative: — 20 dB.

The third point about the decibel is that it works to a logarithmic rather than to a linear scale. In òther words, each time the ear detects a doubling of sound, the intensity has actually gone up by a factor of ten, i.e. ten times the original level for the first doubling, one hundred times for the second, one thousand for the third, and so on.

Now let us examine the way in which values are expressed in decibels, with respect to ratios of sound intensity and sound pressure.

Sound intensity is really the input energy to a device whereas **sound pressure** is effectively the output—what we hear. Each time the intensity is doubled the value goes up by 3dB, whereas each time the pressure is doubled the value goes up by 6dB.

A ratio of intensity that was 100:1 could be written as 10^2:1. Ignoring the :1, we would take the square factor and multiply by ten to express this ratio in decibels -20dB. Thus a ratio of intensity of 1000:1 would be 10^3:1 or 30dB and so on.

For sound pressure the same exercise still applies but the multiplying factor is 20. Thus 100:1 becomes 10^2:1, becomes 2 x 20 = 40 = 40dB, 1000:1 becomes 10^3:1, becomes 3 x 20 = 60 = 60dB.

There are two other units of the measurement of loudness - the phon and the sone. These take into account the fact that the ear does not respond evenly to all frequencies. We will not be concerned with these in our work but they are mentioned here merely to indicate their position in the picture.

The Ends of the Chain

Now we have dealt with the way that sound is generated and we have reviewed the vocabulary of terms we shall meet throughout the book. Now let us turn to two elements closest to us and vital parts of the sound chain - the voice and the ear.

The Human Voice

Human beings generate sounds by means of their vocal chords which intercept air exhaled from the lungs and vibrate to produce a note. The sound must then pass through the pharynx, the mouth and the nose and it is the way in which these cavities are used that determines the tone of the sound we hear and enables us to differentiate one voice from another.

When selecting loudspeakers and operating tone controls it is important to understand the range of frequencies produced by the human voice. The usual fundamental frequency for males is about 125HZ, and about

210HZ for females. This would be a normal voice level, but the trained voices of actors have higher values of about 140HZ and 230HZ respectively.

The **frequency range** of trained voices is unsurprisingly wider than that of untrained voices and males usually have a wider range than females—although female voices are purer, having fewer harmonics (one reason why they tend to make better announcers than men). The pitch of the voice is usually raised in emotional moments and when working in chorus. Here are the frequency ranges of the various parts of our speech:-

Table 1

fundamentals	125-250HZ
vowels	350-2000HZ
consonants	1500-4000HZ

thus the speech area can be concentrated within the 350-4000HZ band, but a wider band would produce more realism, say one of 60-6000HZ. We shall see later that in the case of sound reinforcement systems, it is occasionally desirable to be able to raise the lower frequency limit to reduce **howlround (feedback)**.

Here are the frequency ranges of the fundamentals of singers:-

Table 2

bass	85-340HZ
baritone	90-380HZ
tenor	125-460HZ
alto	130-680HZ
contralto	180-600HZ
soprano	225-1100HZ

In the case of performers it is important that they understand not only the necessity of voice training, but also correct microphone technique. Adequate breath control helps sustain the ends of words, where the vital consonants are often situated. Lose these and clarity suffers. Singers' voices often strain to produce adequate loudness at the high and low frequencies. Gutteral or strident sounds result. Microphone technique can often help. The performer is there to produce the sound. The sound system is there to amplify this and transmit it to the audience; the two must learn to work with each other. Distortion produced by working too loudly into the microphone can only be removed by a lot of expensive electronics.

It is interesting that in the frequency range 62.5—500Hz is found 60% of the human voice's power but only 5% of the intelligibility; in the 500-1000Hz range there is 35% of the power and 35% of the intelligibility but in the 1000-8000Hz range only 5% of the power but 60% of the intelligibility. We shall see later that the tone controls on many simple sound mixers lie outside this last range and therefore cannot directly affect the quality of the voice. This is why it is so important to select a mixer with more comprehensive tone control.

Now let us look at the sound pressure level that the human voice can produce. These are the values measured at a distance of 10'(3m)

Table 3

whisper	30 dBA
conversation	50 dBA
lecturer	60 dBA
actor	70 dBA

We have mentioned that the ear is not equally sensitive to all frequencies. A sound pressure level meter which hears in the same way as we do is said to be following an 'A' weighting, hence the above measurements are made on such a meter. From this we can see that it would be uncomfortable to have to listen to a performance where the sound level was lower than 50 dBA for any considerable length of time. Ideally it should be higher. The precise level is not only a product of the original level and the distance of the listener from the actor, but also of the **ambient noise**.

This is the level of the background noise made up of air conditioning, traffic and of the audience itself. In practical terms it is expensive to silence plant and traffic, and therefore most multipurpose establishments have noise levels in the order of 40 dBA. There are some noisy establishments in the author's experience in the order of 65 dBA! The desired level has been calculated, and forms part of a national series of suggestions for different types of buildings and uses called **Noise Criteria** or NC. The level suggested relates to specific frequency bands, but the average levels for concert halls, theatres, lecture and conference halls is 30 dBA.

We can therefore see that the sound level of the performance must be somewhat higher, say by at least 10dB, than that of the ambient noise. Since we know that the sound pressure level falls 6dB with each doubling of the distance we can calculate how far from an actor the SPL will fall to an unacceptable amount. If we assume the actor is producing 70dB at 10′ then this is 64dB at 20′, 58dB at 40′ and 52dB at 80′. If the ambient noise level in the theatre is 40dB and we need 10dB of difference then we will be in trouble further than 80′ away from the actor and might need reinforcement by a sound system.

In fact these figures should only be used as a guide, since the 6dB rule takes no account of that sound which does not die away but continues to bounce or reverberate around the theatre. This adds to the SPL at some distance from the actor, so that the actual level is higher at this point. It is possible to calculate at which distance the reverberant level begins to add to that of the direct level, and this might indicate that amplification is needed since the reverberant level would, in extreme cases, hinder the intelligibility. Nevertheless the 6dB rule is a good guide for most auditoria. We will see later how different signals are added together to calculate the SPL, say from two or more loudspeakers. It has been found that a contour can be drawn for the human voice, which like most sources is more directional at some frequencies than others, notably those produced in front of the body.

It may be seen from above that the distance from the performer to the perimeter, for an acceptable speech level, must vary with the level produced by him. Nevertheless—if we ignore quality for a moment—people behind the actor but within the line will hear better than those in front but outside the line. Much of the clarity at the upper frequencies is lost on those behind. A vital point to remember when placing people on platforms at meetings.

In the case of performances, actors relate to each other—and so the voice contour may be used to shape the optimum area of hearing in an auditorium.

Decide what sound level is likely to be produced—i.e. trained or untrained speech, and calculate how far away the most acceptable hearing point will be. Scale the template accordingly. People outside that line will not hear satisfactorily without help.

This is where the sound reinforcement system, and the correct acoustic design of the auditorium, can help.

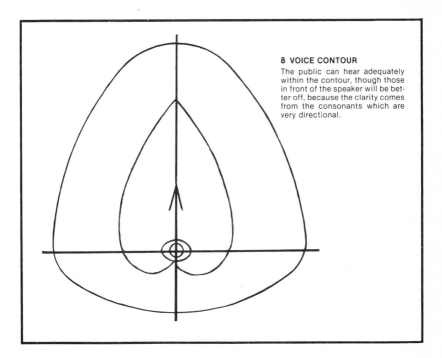

8 VOICE CONTOUR
The public can hear adequately within the contour, though those in front of the speaker will be better off, because the clarity comes from the consonants which are very directional.

Adaptable theatre with all seats within the range of voice (St. Mary's Training College, Twickenham).

The Human Ear

Sound enters the ear and travels down the auditory canal to the ear drum, which vibrates. These sensations are passed to the hearing nerves by other mechanisms in the inner ear. It is the size of the auditory canal that determines how sensitive the ear is to various frequencies.

Most young people can detect, under ideal conditions, pure tones of 16—20,000 Hz and this range diminishes with age, especially at the upper end. The ear is more sensitive in the range 1000—6000 Hz. Should we require a sound either above or below this band to sound as loud as a frequency in that band, we should have to amplify it more.

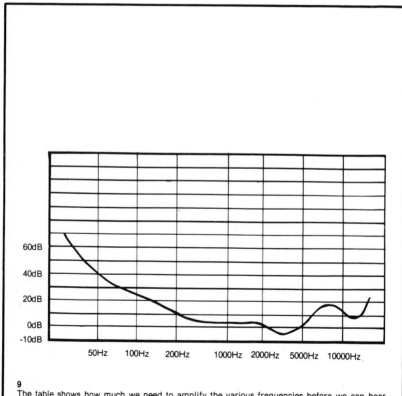

9
The table shows how much we need to amplify the various frequencies before we can hear them. The ear is not equally sensitive at all frequencies. A 50Hz tone would need to be amplified 40dB before it appeared as loud as a 1000Hz tone.

The ear can detect a very wide range of sound pressure levels. At the reference frequency of 1000Hz the quietest level the ear can detect is set as OdB although the ear is actually most sensitive in the range 3kHz to 5kHz, achieving a level of—4dB.

The loudest sound, without actually incurring permanent damage, is about a million times greater at 120 dB.

Under ideal conditions the minimum change in intensity which the ear can detect is about 1dB.

10 SOUND PRESSURE LEVELS FOR SOME COMMON NOISES

130 dB	
	threshold of pain
120 dB	
	loud rock music
110 dB	
	underground train
100 dB	heavy lorry
	loud classical music
90 dB	heavy street traffic
80 dB	average factory
70 dB	noisy office
	actor
60 dB	lecturer
	average office
50 dB	street
	conversation
40 dB	soft music
30 dB	quiet theatre
	whisper
20 dB	sound studio
10 dB	rustling leaves
	anechoic room
0 dB	threshold of hearing at 1kHz

High Sound Levels and Deafness

It is certain that prolonged exposure to a high sound level produces a temporary loss of hearing and that continuation would lead to permanent damage.

The damage is done to the nerves of the inner ear and, on occasions, to the auditory nerve. It is irreversible by surgery. Initially the effect is on the higher frequencies but extends in severe cases over the whole spectrum.

The problem relating to performers is that considerably more research has been carried out on the effects of industrial sound levels than on musical sound levels. These tables indicate the maximum exposure in industry for the U.K. and the U.S.A. and it should be noted that they are measured in slightly different ways. The U.K. 'A' scale corresponds to the response of the human ear—the U.S.A. 'OSHA' scale is more concerned with linear exposure to continuous sound levels:-

Table 4	under 90 dBA	no limit
U.K. (A)	90 dBA	8 hours per day maximum
	93 dBA	4 hours per day maximum
	96 dBA	2 hours per day maximum
	99 dBA	1 hour per day maximum
	102 dBA	½ hour per day maximum
	105 dBA	¼ hour per day maximum
USA (OSHA)	90 dBA	8 hours per day maximum
(1970)	95 dBA	4 hours per day maximum
	100 dBA	2 hours per day maximum
	105 dBA	1 hour per day maximum
	110 dBA	½ hour per day maximum
	115 dBA	¼ hour per day maximum
	over 115 dBA	none.

Since Rock bands are quite capable of producing sound levels well in excess of 100 dBA, these tables would suggest that many musicians and their followers must be suffering. Unfortunately the above criteria cannot apply with certainty to music since it is not classified as a continuous noise—the definition is that the sound level should not fluctuate by more than 8 dBA, and music usually does.

Nevertheless, it is well known that some rock musicians are now suffering from deafness and it is likely that others exposed, for similar times, to comparable levels—such as studio engineers and road crew—might also be suffering.

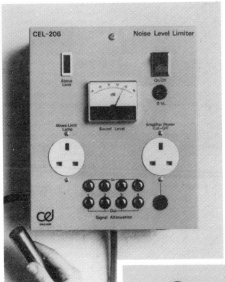

The CEL 206 noise level limiter for monitoring and attenuating excessively loud entertainment noise.

A hand held meter for measuring the sound pressure level at various frequencies.

Some licencing authorities have attempted to limit sound pressure level at concerts when granting licences but have frequently chosen levels and measurement criteria which are exceeded by other events under their control, such as football crowds and opera performances (a trained opera singer can produce sound levels well in excess of 100 dBA).

The authorities have subsequently attempted to achieve some realism by imposing an average level and a higher peak level, both of which should not be exceeded. Typical limits might be an average level of 90 dBA and a peak level of 105 dBA. Some limited research into disco sound has been carried out in Leeds and this suggests that a frequent visitor to a disco could suffer some hearing loss in the speech frequencies later in life. The criteria for the research was based on a frequency of visits of once a month or more and in circumstances where the peak noise level frequently reached 128 dBA. This would suggest that the criteria of industrial noise should be apply to music but more research is needed before this could be stated with certainty. Meanwhile it is obviously prudent to err on the side of safety.

However, such limited research that has been carried out suggests that it is not the audience who need protection, it is the performers and their staff!

Summary
Section One will be valuable as a reference throughout the book but the basics should not be missed . . .
Vibrations per second are the frequency which is expressed as Hz, the first vibration being the fundamental, subsequent multiple vibrations being harmonics. Music has a very wide frequency range, speech has a limited range. High frequency sounds are more directional than low frequency sounds.

The decibel is a unit of comparison between two other measurements—one of which may be an agreed standard reference.

The level of sound in auditoria is measured as sound pressure level—SPL—and is expressed as dB with OdB being the agreed limit of hearing for reference at a frequency of 1000Hz.

Section Two

Acoustics

To many people, acoustics are only of concern in concert halls; some go as far as to suggest that ordinary halls don't have acoustics at all!

The next section breaks down the different elements we are concerned with in designing auditoria. Even though our prime concern here is the design of sound systems, it is vital to understand how these systems will behave in a given space.

Reverberation
Electro-Acoustic Reverberation
Reflections and Reflectors
The Grazing Effect—Seating Layout
Absorption and Insulation
The Orchestral Area
Auditorium Shape
Structural Alterations

and their terminology . . .

Reverberation

When a sound is produced in an auditorium, it continues to be heard for some time after it has been cut off. This is the result of the sound bouncing round the walls of the auditorium before reaching the listener and this process is known as **reverberation**.

Just how much is heard at this point depends not only on the strength of the original sound but also on the size and shape of the auditorium and upon how it is furnished. A large auditorium is likely to have more reverberation than a small one. Similarly, soft furnishings absorb some frequencies more than hard surfaces, so less sound is reflected back into the auditorium.

It is therefore possible to conceive of an auditorium being reverberant or **'lively'**, or non-reverberant or **'dead'**.

In acoustical work, it is necessary to identify the amount of reverberation present in an auditorium so as to be able to communicate whether, and by how much, it is lively or dead. This is done by measuring the time a specific sound takes to die away to one millionth of its intensity.

This may be written as a ratio 1,000,000:1 or 10^6:1 and we may remember from earlier that this leads us to express it as 60 dB.

It may be understood from the above that reverberation extends the effect of a single sound. This might be desirable in music but is most certainly not so in speech, where the result will be blurred and unintelligible dialogue. Some sounds suffer more than others—vowels are especially liable to be obscured by the delay on preceding strong consonants. So we can see that an auditorium which has an ideal **reverberation time** (RT) for music will not be ideal for speech, and vice - versa.

Let us look at music first. It has been suggested that different forms of music require a different RT—for example classical and modern music usually need a shorter RT than choral work. So again, even within the music 'umbrella', there are conflicting requirements for designers of multi-purpose auditoria.

Earlier we said that reverberation was related to the size of the auditorium and it is possible to assess the desired RT by selecting the volume on the following graph. The diagram also indicates the RT of some well known venues and it is interesting to compare the times for music with the times for speech. The RT differs at each frequency but if the measured frequency is not stated then it is assumed to be 500Hz. The attendance is also important and should ideally be stated. If the seating is not absorbent a full auditorium can have an RT as much as half a second lower than it did when it was empty. This often overlooked fact has caused much dismay to musicians who rehearse in empty halls.

In the case of the design of new buildings the desired RT can be built up from creating the appropriate volume. This can itself be suggested by an averaged figure per seat. There is some dispute over the ideal figures but the volume per seat for music should be between 4.5 and 7.4 cubic metres (160 and 260 cubic feet) with 5.7 cubic metres as the best option (200 cubic feet). The figures for speech range from 2.3 to 4.3 cubic metres (80 to 150 cubic feet) with 3.1 cubic metres as the best option (110 cubic feet). The precise volume depends on the use, the kind of music involved and the balance with the amount of speech involved.

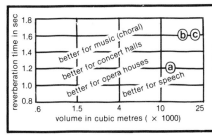

a   Covent Garden Opera House 1.2 (12,240 cu m)
b   Free Trade Hall Manchester 1.6 (15,500 cu m)
c   Royal Festival Hall London 1.6 (22,000 cu m)
    Royal Albert Hall London 2.9 (86,600 cu m)

TABLE 5
reverberation times with volume

It may be remembered that reverberation is concerned with reflected sound and we shall see later how these reflections behave in detail, but for the present it is important to note that some reflections can be used to enhance the sound, for both speech and music. In the case of the latter, the design is made easy since the orchestra will most certainly be located in the same place (in respect to the audience) on each occasion.

In the case of speech, it is likely that the actor/lecturer/audience relationship will alter and this makes the use of reflected sound more difficult.

It can be clearly seen therefore that, in purely architectural terms, the design of a good acoustic for multipurpose use is extremely complex. It is therefore pertinent to relate electronics to this problem and we shall see later how sound systems may cater for different reverberation times within the same auditorium.

In the case of an existing building the RT can obviously be measured by producing a **point sound**, like a gunshot, and measuring the time it takes to decay by 60dB. But in the case of a new building, or one being altered, the RT has to be calculated.

This is done by considering the dimensions of the auditorium with respect to the amount of sound its surfaces will absorb. We will take a closer look at absorption later, especially at the influence that the audience has on sound.

There are, in fact, several ways of calculating the RT and the use of computers has led to the discovery that these formulae are not as accurate as was once thought. Several modern concert halls have RT shorter than was originally expected and have resorted to electronics to overcome the problem. The discrepancies arise because the calculations' constant values are sometimes relatively inaccurate, and the equations do not take into account the behaviour of sound waves nor the location of the different absorbing surfaces within the room.

In simple terms we may summarise this area by saying that speech requires a less lively acoustic than music and that, electronic means aside, this may be achieved by introducing sound-absorbing elements into the auditorium—curtains, carpets, and people being the easiest to obtain.

Electro-Acoustic Reverberation

We now know that the reverberation time has a direct effect on the quality of the music or speech presented.

In the case of both speech and music, if the RT is too long then absorbents can be introduced into the auditorium. Should the RT be too short a different system has to be employed, and this is where electro-acoustics come in. Basically there are two systems—**ambiophony**—and **assisted resonance.**

Not suprisingly these systems are most often located in auditoria where music is the prime content. The most famous example of assisted resonance is the work of P. H. Parkin at the Royal Festival Hall. Other systems can be found at York University, Hexagon Centre Reading and numerous auditoria on the continent.

The basic difference in the two systems is that ambiophony technique employs a few microphones placed close to the source of sound. These are then fed to delay units, usually producing four alternate times, relevant to

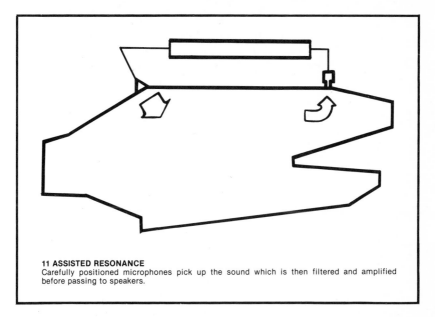

11 ASSISTED RESONANCE
Carefully positioned microphones pick up the sound which is then filtered and amplified before passing to speakers.

the length of the auditorium—and thence to sets of loudspeakers positioned in the auditorium ceiling appropriate to the amount of delay given.

Some reservations about this method have been expressed with regard to feedback generated by the close miking; it seems that the system may suit some acoustics and presentations, but not all.

The assisted resonance systems is more complex. This places numerous microphones strategically in the ceiling, mounted in specially resonant boxes. The sound is then filtered to emerge from many loudspeakers mounted again in the ceiling.

Reflections and Reflectors

Whenever a sound is produced in an auditorium, whether it is a live one from actor or instrument, or an amplified one via a loudspeaker, a certain portion of the sound will not reach the audience directly but will be reflected from the walls, ceilings and other surfaces in the auditorium.

Reflections can be harmful where they arrive at the listener after the direct sound and blur the words, or they may be useful where they combine with the direct sound to improve volume and intelligibility.

So it is important to consider how sound is reflected and how it should be controlled.

It is possible to determine what reflections will be produced by sounds striking different surfaces. Consider a concave surface, such as might be found in auditoria, domes, circle fronts and rear walls. There the **reflected sound** is concentrated by the surface, so that some people could experience a blurring of the original sound and even a distinct echo. The most famous example of this phenomenon is the Royal Albert Hall dome, where the problem was somewhat overcome by the suspension of 'flying saucers' to prevent the direct sound reaching the concave surface.

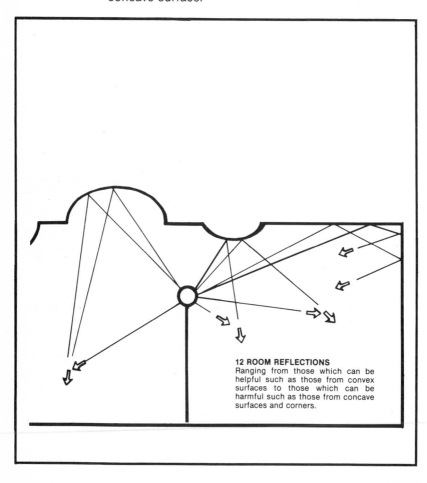

12 ROOM REFLECTIONS
Ranging from those which can be helpful such as those from convex surfaces to those which can be harmful such as those from concave surfaces and corners.

13 DOME ECHOES

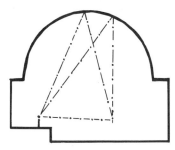 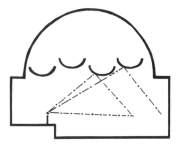

The drawing (left) shows how the dome of the Royal Albert Hall focuses the sound and reflects it back into the audience where it arrives so late as to be heard as a distant echo.

Here the 'flying saucers' prevent the sound from reaching the dome and it is reflected to enhance the direct sound.

An excellent shot of the Royal Albert Hall during a television broadcast; the picture clearly shows the "flying saucers" suspended in the dome.

This is perhaps an extreme example but it serves to illustrate the point. In most situations the culprit is likely to be a curved rear wall. The radius of the curve will determine where the reflected sound is concentrated and it may be that the artists on stage suffer more than the audience. In this case the problem should not be dismissed merely because the paying patrons are not directly affected. They will be indirectly affected by the result of the sound on the performer.

One aspect of the concave shape which has to be considered is the radius of the curve and its relationship to wavelength. The distance across the arc gives a direct indication of the frequencies affected. For example a curved back wall of 20M (65.5') will focus sounds down the range—provided that it is not obstructed by balconies nor covered with heavy absorbent material. Even if it is obstructed it may still reflect higher frequency sounds. The same principle applies in reverse to small arcs like ceiling cornices which reflect only high frequency sounds.

The answer, in auditorium design, is to ensure that the focal point of any curve lies outside not only the audience but also the stage area too. Many stages suffer from disastrous back echoes because the architect forgot the performers.

On the other hand convex surfaces will disperse the sound and this may prove helpful if the dispersal can reinforce the direct non-reflected sound waves.

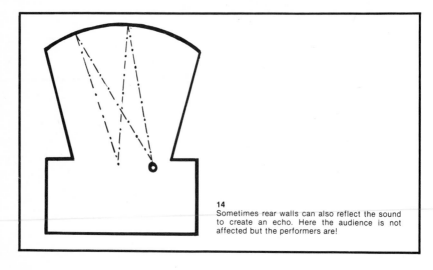

14
Sometimes rear walls can also reflect the sound to create an echo. Here the audience is not affected but the performers are!

This is the basic principle behind the reflectors often seen above concert platforms or modern theatre orchestra pits.

The size of the reflector is important because it relates to the wavelength of the sounds involved. It is of no value merely to fix the size in relationship to what looks good. The reflector must be larger than ¼ of the wavelength of a specific frequency otherwise the sound will bend round the edge and not as much will be reflected. It must be clear that a certain amount of this bending—known as **edge diffraction**—is inevitable anyway in view of the long wavelengths of the lower frequencies, but it will be recalled that the upper frequencies are the more important for speech.

Moving away from useful reflections and back to harmful ones again—one problem often found in the rectangular multi-purpose hall is that of corner reflections. These occur where the sound hits the ceiling, or the underside of a balcony, and is reflected back towards the audience via the rear wall. This problem is particularly acute at the high frequency (short wavelength) sounds and wall or ceiling treatment is again desirable to absorb or disperse the sound.

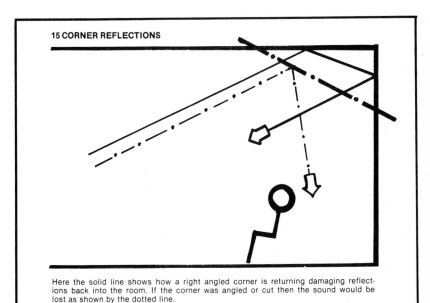

15 CORNER REFLECTIONS

Here the solid line shows how a right angled corner is returning damaging reflections back into the room. If the corner was angled or cut then the sound would be lost as shown by the dotted line.

Another kind of damaging reflection frequently found in rectangular or parallel areas is that of **standing waves**. These are accentuations of certain frequencies whose wavelength is an exact multiple of one of the auditorium's basic dimensions. The accent is placed on a frequency only in parts of the auditorium but this can give rise to feedback **if** a microphone needs to be placed in that position. The system then becomes more sensitive to that frequency.

In auditoria already constructed, one solution is to insert a filter into the sound chain to de-emphasise the problem frequency. This may have to be done several times and we shall look at this process in more detail later. Another aid is to provide more absorption on the offending surfaces to cut down the reflection.

In the planning of a new building great care must be taken with absorption and reflection. Parallel walls also need attention since they can cause problems although they are often the easiest design option. We shall see later that they can be useful to enhance the quality of music but where speech use predominates, the walls cause **'flutter echoes'** which greatly impede intelligibility. The echoes are caused by the audience sounds, coughing and programme rustling, bouncing back and forth across the auditorium without any chance of being dispersed.

The walls should therefore be slightly angled so that the sound path is dispersed towards the rear of the auditorium where it can reinforce other sound paths. In an existing building the problem can be over come by providing some absorption to the wall surface although of course this will alter the reverberation time. Another method, which can be adopted with some absorption treatment if neccesary, is to attach panels to the wall which are each at a slight angle to the main surface. These act as small reflectors again dispersing the sound towards the rear.

In a building that is being planned, the answer is to avoid parallel surfaces and take care with dispersion and absorption.

The auditorium therefore has to be carefully designed so that the reflected sound in all areas is either helpful to the main sound or is absorbed. Convex surfaces are useful to disperse and reflect desirable sounds, concave surfaces may lead to harmful echoes and parallel surfaces are to be avoided where speech intelligibility is of paramount importance.

Ceiling reflector panels at the Abbey Theatre Dublin, lowered for work on the lighting bars, may be angled to adjust the acoustics.

The Grazing Effect—Seating Layout

Earlier we saw how the sound level decreased as we went further away from the source of sound. There are a number of factors which affect this situation such as the interference from reflected sound and the effect of the type of source itself, but the basic principle holds true.

Obviously the closer that the audience are to the stage then the better they should hear, because the direct sound will not have so far to travel. However much of the strength of the sound is being absorbed by the audience **(the grazing effect)** itself and one way to overcome this is to remove the obstruction—raise each row above the previous on the tiered or raking principle. The sightlines are also improved by this method and ideally the seats should be staggered so that one person looks between the heads of those in front

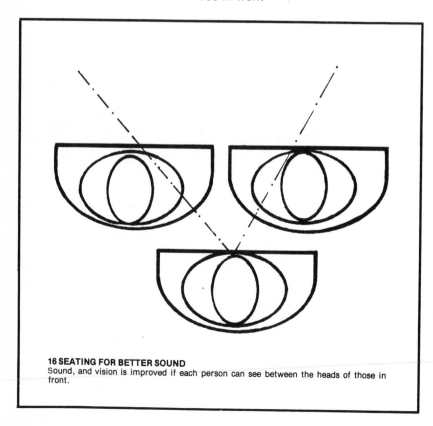

16 SEATING FOR BETTER SOUND
Sound, and vision is improved if each person can see between the heads of those in front.

Improving the sight and sound for the rear seats.

The rear rows will need a higher tier or rake than those in front to preserve the benefit, and the circle and balcony levels will need the highest increase that is permissible under the licensing regulations.

In multi-purpose auditoria where the stalls floor often has to be flat to cater for sports, dances and exhibitions, great consideration should be given to the provision of either rostra or retractable seating for the rear rows where the effect of distance and absorption will be most felt.

Absorption and Insulation

These two terms are often confused with each other so we will deal with them side by side for comparison.

Sound Absorption is the term used to cover the process whereby the surfaces of the auditorium reflect different amounts of sound at different frequencies dependent upon the treatment of the surface. You may remember that we have said broadly that hard surfaces reflect (do not absorb) as much sound as soft surfaces. The amount of absorption has a direct bearing on the reverberation.

Sound Insulation is the term used to cover the process of preventing sound from one area intruding into another. The most effective kind of insulation is weight.

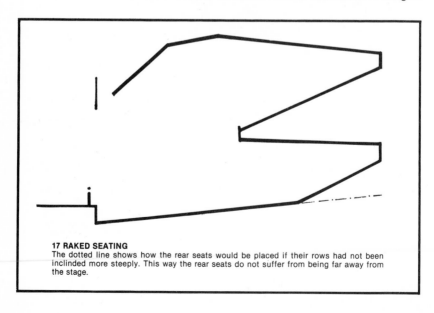

17 RAKED SEATING
The dotted line shows how the rear seats would be placed if their rows had not been inclinded more steeply. This way the rear seats do not suffer from being far away from the stage.

There is an incorrect but often repeated theory that sound absorbing tiles will prevent sound from being passed from one area to another. The tiles will certainly help to reduce the reverberation in the area and thus limit the amount of sound likely to pass into the other area, but only proper insulation will really be effective. The calculations for both insulation and absorption are complex and there are for absorption (related to reverberation) several equations dependent upon the purpose behind the result. The most common formula developed by W. C. Sabine in the late 19th century is:-

$$\text{Reverberation Time} = \frac{0.16 \ (\text{constant}) \ \times \ \text{volume } M^3}{\text{total absorption in } M^2 \ \text{sabin units.}}$$

The **sabin** is a unit of absorption and values are available for building and furnishing materials. In fact several values are given since the absorption varies with the frequency. Were the absorption to be total then the coefficient would be 1 and conversely were no sound to be absorbed then the value would be 0. Here are some common values:-

Table 6
ABSORPTION COEFFICIENTS

	250Hz	500Hz	1000Hz
Brickwork	0.04	0.02	0.04
Concrete	0.02	0.02	0.04
Plaster solid backing	0.03	0.02	0.03
Carpet, thick pile	0.25	0.5	0.5
Air (per Cu M)	nil	nil	0.003
Audience in seat upholstered	0.4	0.46	0.46
Wooden seat, empty		0.15	
Rostrum per m²	0.1	nil	nil

It should be noted that these, and other materials, have in fact several frequency bands of coefficients. The ones here are shown in simpler form for illustration rather than for the basis of calculations.

... It is worth noting that there is no definitive table of absorption coefficients since different acousticians and laboratories have used varying techniques to achieve measurements. The differences however are slight and are not relevant in the kind of broad calculations we are discussing in this book.

The use of computers in acoustics has determined that the reverberation/absorption calculations are not as accurate as was once thought since they do not take into account either the location of the various absorbing surfaces in the auditorium or the way in which sound is diffused. Until an alternative is proven however, the above sabine formula will be adequate. The formula is only altered where the calculations involve large auditoria and where the air has an absorption factor too. The formula then appears thus:-

$$\text{Reverberation Time} = \frac{0.16 \ (\text{constant}) \times \text{volume m}^2}{\text{Absorption M}^2 \ \text{sabins} + \text{XV}}$$

Where V is room volume in M^2
X is air coefficient

Where imperial measurements are involved the constant changes thus . . .

$$\text{Reverberation Time} = \frac{0.05 \ (\text{constant}) \times \text{volume in cubic feet}}{\text{Absorption in square feet sabins} \times \text{volume} \times \text{air coefficient}}$$

It can be seen from Table 6 that hard surfaces absorb less sound than soft surfaces and hence they are good reflectors. For example at 500Hz brick, concrete or plaster absorbs only 2% of the sound whereas carpet absorbs 50%. The thickness of the surface is important, especially with soft furnishing such as carpets; thin felt on concrete absorbs only 25% at 500Hz, whereas thick pile on concrete absorbs 50% at the same frequency. Hence it is possible to achieve some comfort in the furnishing without seriously lowering the RT.

More absorption is achieved if the substance is placed some distance away from the wall so that an air gap is formed. The actual distance is critical, a gap of 1½" provides up to 10dB less absorption at 500Hz than does a gap of 6".

Should this principle be taken further so that individual cavities are formed - called **Helmholtz resonators** ·then specific frequencies can be absorbed very well although others in the range are not, so these are useful for dealing with troublesome frequencies.

The treatment of the surface is also important for example a porous brick surface can have its absorption lowered by 15% by one coat of paint applied with roller, or raised by 20% if one coat is applied by brush. (These figures at 500Hz).

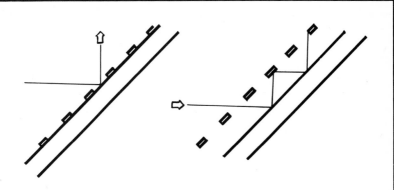

18 WALL SURFACES
The drawing on the right shows how sound loses much of its energy behind the cavity. This surface is more absorbent than the one on the left. The dimensions are not arbitrary but relate to the precise frequency or frequencies which need more absorption than others.

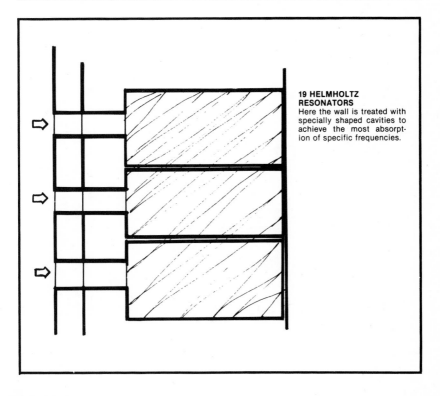

19 HELMHOLTZ RESONATORS
Here the wall is treated with specially shaped cavities to achieve the most absorption of specific frequencies.

Suppose that the reverberation time of an existing room was considered too long and it was desired to shorten it. This could be achieved by introducing more absorption, although decreasing the size would also achieve the same result but one presumes that reduction in seating capacity is not desirable on a permanent basis. Nevertheless several theatres now have lowering ceilings to cut off upper circles if they are not used, others separate parts of the auditorium with partitions or curtains.

But in an area where these are not possible only absorption will do. However it should be borne in mind that for each 3dB reduction in reverberant sound, the absorption has to double. This might not be difficult to achieve in a multi-purpose hall but would be in a traditional red plush and gilt theatre.

The lowering ceiling at London's Piccadilly Theatre viewed from the Upper Circle. Although this particular ceiling does not form a complete acoustic seal it alters the ambiance of the theatre considerably.

Nottingham Playhouse showing the absorbent wall treatment of timber slats.

Now let us turn to sound insulation. As far as the theatre manager is concerned we may define the problem as the prevention of undesirable sounds from reaching the auditorium.

The design of the building is, of course, itself a major factor but that is a study for a separate book.

Firstly it must be appreciated that in insulation the 'weak link' theory predominates again—for example, a thick wall will be far less effective if penetrated by doors and windows. Unless these are in use they should be bricked up—simple boarding is not sufficient though some slight improvement would occur.

Where there is no alternative but to leave doors and windows in use then some treatment is necessary. In the case of windows a fixed frame will be a better insulator than an opening one and, of course, double glazing also helps a great deal although the air gap should be at least 200 mm for there to be any benefit. Heavier glass, more panes and a greater air gap is better still. Doors should be examined to ensure that they close properly—gaps can let through much sound, but the only real solution is an air lock.

Areas surrounding the main auditorium should be as absorbent as possible—carpets, curtains, tiles etc., to cut down the reverberant sound—curtains are especially useful anyway to improve decor and carpets help cushion the impact sound, like high heels, which travels through the structure.

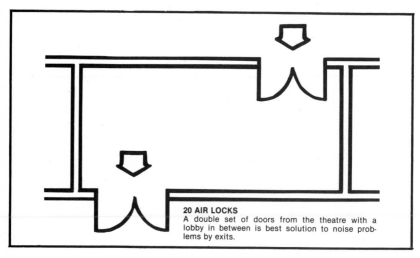

20 AIR LOCKS
A double set of doors from the theatre with a lobby in between is best solution to noise problems by exits.

Any membrane, such as a door or wall, effects some reduction to the level of the sound passing through it, and since this can be calculated, it is possible to indicate how thick a membrane should be, and of what it should be constructed in order to achieve the desired reduction. The actual amount of reduction varies with the frequency but using averages for examples, a standard 4″ (100mm) brick wall with plaster both sides, effects a reduction of about 40dB. Therefore if the theatre is encompassed by such walls and the sound pressure level attendant on the theatre side of the wall is say 80dB then the sound pressure level on the other side will be about 40dB. We are however not quite so concerned about sound coming out of the theatre as we are about sound getting in, perhaps from other neighbouring venues or from adjacent roads or railways. A table of other membranes and their reduction indices is given in the appendix.

Heating and Ventilation are subjects for another book but as far as sound systems are concerned the general principle is that the noise near a duct or grille is substantially higher than elsewhere so all grilles should be placed well away from the audience. A common problem occurs when the use of a theatre changes, requiring a lower background noise level than that which was acceptable when the building originally opened. Under these circumstances it is not realistic to install a new system and hence the answer is usually to fit silencers to the grilles and perhaps in extreme cases lower the speed of the system or even switch if off altogther during actual curtain up times, using it only before the show and during the interval.

To summarise—insulation deals with preventing sound being transmitted and is best achieved by weight. Absorption deals with the reflection of sounds by the design of surfaces and is based on the fact that different substances absorb different amounts of sound at various frequencies.

The Orchestral Area
Where any work involves the contribution of several players, be it opera, concert or light entertainment, it is fundamental that the area housing those players must receive careful consideration. We shall deal with two types—the stage performance by an orchestra and the orchestra pit.

Earlier we talked of a given reverberation time being more suitable for one kind of music than another and there is a direct parallel in the orchestra pit.

The Italian opera houses favoured for Mozart have large open orchestra pits and this is ideal for small orchestras and in well orchestrated works where the singers are not overpowered. However, a large orchestra, such as that required for Wagner, may indeed be too loud by comparison with the singers if left completely in the open. The solution therefore is to partially enclose the pit by placing part of it under the stage. This is believed to have been introduced by Wagner himself at the opera house he designed at Bayreuth.

In more recent times, modern musicals such as 'Jesus Christ Superstar' totally enclosed the pit in perspex so that the sound was competely under the control of the sound engineer through microphones on each instrument. This enables not only the balance of one instrument against another to be controlled, but also the volume. It must be agreed that the conductor is denied this kind of instant control, yet it is often necessary today with works conceived in or popularised by recording studios.

Generally then, the pit should be large enough to accommodate many players. If opera and ballet are envisaged this might mean at least 60 musicians but for most light entertainment work 30 would be a maximum. It has been suggested that a player should be accommodated within between 1^2M and 1.5^2M. The pit should be designed to blend the sound in the correct balance with the sound of the performers on stage. It is advisable to plan for later additions of acoustic treatment to the walls and ceiling—it is easier to add panels than to take them away, although acoustics that would please one musician are unlikely to please another. The sightlines from musician to conductor are important, and lifts combined with rostra are essential.

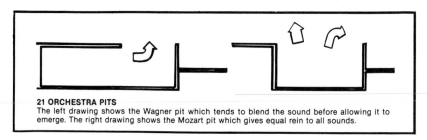

21 ORCHESTRA PITS
The left drawing shows the Wagner pit which tends to blend the sound before allowing it to emerge. The right drawing shows the Mozart pit which gives equal rein to all sounds.

Of course, for many people, an orchestra pit is a luxury and they have to content themselves with fencing off part of the auditorium floor. This introduces two dangers: firstly, the pit as a whole is now higher than normal and might intrude into the sightlines of the stalls. Secondly, the whole orchestra is now clearly into the acoustic of the audience and could well have more prominence than the performers on stage who have few reflectors to help them. Many complaints of bands being too loud occur in this situation.

The solution is obviously not easy, short of physical alterations. The pit itself, floor and walls should be lined with as much absorbent material as possible. Trial and error will tell which areas need more than others—brass and timpani are certainly candidates. Alternatively, the production might allow for the orchestra to be placed on stage, where there are more absorbents, although care needs to be taken with performers' mics picking up the band. We shall deal with this situation later.

In more serious works, concerts and the like, the orchestra are always on stage. Since we are concerned with theatre we will not deal here with the design of the concert platform, but theatres and multi-purpose halls frequently stage concerts so we shall look more closely at the problems.

The central problem is that of absorption. Placed on stage among drapes and scenery the reverberation time is lower, and much is lost to the cavernous fly-tower above. The requirement is to make the stage acoustic at one with the auditorium. The orchestra should be as far

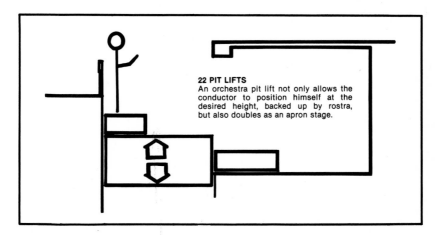

22 PIT LIFTS
An orchestra pit lift not only allows the conductor to position himself at the desired height, backed up by rostra, but also doubles as an apron stage.

downstage as possible and obviously an apron is a distinct advantage here. Next, the rear musicians should be mounted on rostra to improve sightlines and hearing for those at the back of the hall. Attractive though it may be, as far as possible there should be no curtaining involved. If the event is frequent, it would be worth investing in a series of hard reflector flats to form a band 'shell'. The construction of the flats is important since unless they are able to form a wall and remain as separate units then only some frequencies will be reflected—notably the higher ones. The surface should be hardboard or ply—not canvas. Ceiling pieces are easily dealt with in theatres with fly-towers and it is conceivable that the units could be permanently rigged and just dropped in as required. Theatres without flying facilities are not likely to suffer much from the loss of ceiling pieces as there will be no fly-tower and there will therefore be less volume to damage the reverberation time, although the reflections will still be lost of course. If the units are positioned with care and painted the same colour as the auditorium—the illusion of one room, as well as of one acoustic, will be improved.

There are other aspects of orchestral work involving equipment which we will look at later. Meanwhile, let us summarise by saying that the orchestral area is not a backstage facility which can be ignored; it requires as much consideration as the performance itself.

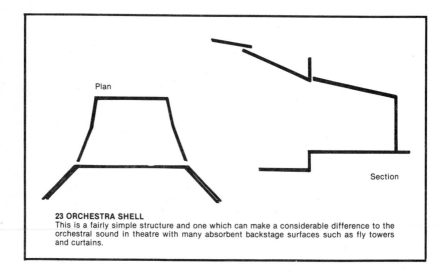

Plan

Section

23 ORCHESTRA SHELL
This is a fairly simple structure and one which can make a considerable difference to the orchestral sound in theatre with many absorbent backstage surfaces such as fly towers and curtains.

Auditorium Shape

Now that we know more of the behaviour of sound waves we may be able to discuss the ideal auditorium shape before going on to some more detailed aspects.

Many theatres are constructed on the fan shaped principle in order to position as many people as possible close to the stage. But this is not a twentieth century idea since the Greeks built Epidaurus this way about 300 BC, and enlarged it to accommodate 14000 people 100 years later. The design is interesting since it suggests the Greeks knew a lot about acoustics—consider the tiering and the grazing effect for example.

In an indoor fan shape the line of walls and ceilings may be considered to be ideal for reflection. But in fact many of the world's successful concert halls are, or were, rectangular—Boston Symphony Hall, Bristol Colston Hall, Vienna Musikvereinssaal, Glasgow St. Andrews Hall, to select just four. They have been considered to have the desirable qualities for music with respect to the dispersion of direct and indirect sound and the sense of involvement created for the audience.

There may be some confusion arising in the reader's mind since we have spoken of the need to avoid parallel surfaces which create flutter echoes and standing waves, but it must be remembered that these buildings are often richly decorated in a way that sound is either dispersed or absorbed. The architect's vocabulary is

The fan-shaped amphitheatre at Epidaurus.

smaller today as far as interior structural decor is concerned and large plain surfaces proliferate. Parallel walls are useful in pure music areas however since they can add fullness to the sound by the wave patterns they help to create, but they should be chosen by acoustic consultant and architect specifically with that in mind, rather than adopted as the easiest design criterion.

The rectangular shape also has historic social connections with parts of the audience being more desirous of seeing each other than of the stage or platform.

One disadvantage of the rectangular concert hall is the flat floor which increases the absorption of sound over the heads of the audience so that back rows often have difficulty in hearing. The reason for the choice of floor is that the concert halls were frequently multi-purpose and also housed dancing and banquets: something many managers today will understand. The benefits to the box office of multi-purpose are often achieved at the expense of the integral nature of each form of entertainment. Compromise often makes an audience uneasy and performers may have to work harder to compensate.

One compromise in stalls seating which has been proven to work is that of combining a flat stalls floor for the first half of the seating and then tiering the remainder—often in phases which have been referred to as vineyard steps.

It is understood that the flat seating is sufficiently close to the stage for the grazing effect to be negligible whilst the tiering at the rear not only improves the acoustics for the audience but the sightlines as well. People have stated that they feel closer to the stage if they can see clearly above the heads of those in front.

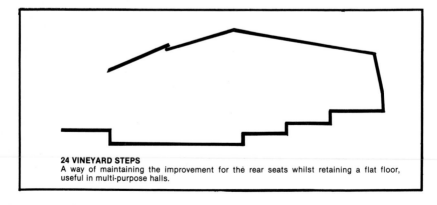

24 VINEYARD STEPS
A way of maintaining the improvement for the rear seats whilst retaining a flat floor, useful in multi-purpose halls.

For multi-purpose auditoria, it is not unreasonable to suggest that the flat floor could be provided with removable seating whilst the tiering could be permanent, rostra or retractable.

It has been suggested that once a certain capacity has been reached, it is better to form an arena—using well tiered rear rows—than to add a balcony. Certainly advantage to the front rows of the balcony is lost on those behind. In order to preserve good tiering in the stalls the balcony may become too steep and in any case the overhang will shorten the reverberation of the sound to those seats as well as making them feel shut off from other parts of the auditorium. Unfortunately a balcony may become essential with very large seating capacities otherwise the back row of the arena would be too far away. Nevertheless the projection should be kept to a minimum.

We may summarise by saying that orchestral needs are traditionally served by rectangular arenas (the parallel walls can add fullness to the tone but need careful design to avoid flutter echoes). Larger capacities than could be reasonably accommodated in a rectangular hall could be met by a fan shape or by adding a balcony, though both cause problems; the former introducing concave surfaces and the latter weakening the stalls tiering. Speech is better in well-absorbed fan-shaped auditoria than in rectangular auditoria, because of the shorter reverberation times and the inherant shape which aids reflections.

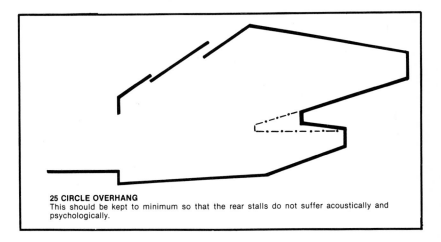

25 CIRCLE OVERHANG
This should be kept to minimum so that the rear stalls do not suffer acoustically and psychologically.

Structural Alterations

All too rarely one reads of money being available for structural improvements to be carried out to an auditorium. At such times the relevant benefits must not obscure the fact that the acoustics will change.

Redecoration schemes frequently remove the drapes that were thought merely decorative until the RT increases, or they are added and the room becomes deader. Lighting slots are cut into ceiling or walls, which adds the volume of the void to that of the main auditorium, changing the RT at certain frequencies. Another problem in the introduction of a void area next to the auditorium is that some insulation will be lost between the auditorium and an adjacent area—the weak link now being the slot itself.

It is important that the RT of the void is less than that of the main auditorium otherwise sound will be heard to reverberate in the void after it has died away in the auditorium. On rare occasions, massive alterations may take place, like extending the balcony or adding a fly-tower, with consequent massive changes in volume and RT. Studies have shown that a fly-tower without absorbent material can add over a second to the reverberation time at lower frequencies.

Sometimes scenery is brought out into apron walls and ceilings, transforming what was once a carefully designed reflector into an absorber.

On all such occasions the acoustics will change—possibly for the better—but consideration of the result should be made first.

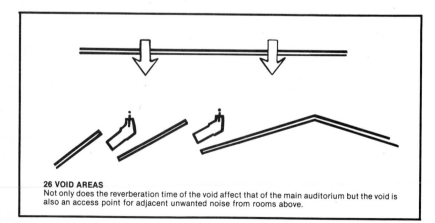

26 VOID AREAS
Not only does the reverberation time of the void affect that of the main auditorium but the void is also an access point for adjacent unwanted noise from rooms above.

A Model RT

We have said that a calculated RT still implies a certain amount of error. If we were concerned with the design of concert halls then this error would be important, and however important the acoustics of theatres and leisure centres are, this error is not something we should become over conscious of in a book of this nature.

It is interesting however to note what work is being done to reduce this error. One way is to produce a scaled down model of the theatre correct in every detail and capable of behaving acoustically as a small version of the real thing. Acoustic tests are carried out and the results scaled up accordingly. Until recently this has been very expensive and thus only justifiable for high performance areas. However research carried out in England has reduced this cost considerably by working to smaller scales. For example the ill-fated Edinburgh Opera House model was costed in 1975 at £12,000.00 and built to a scale of ⅛. The recent models are scaled at 1/50 and cost only £4,000.00. The use of computers is likely to extend progress so that every new building for performances could have prior acoustic test.

A detail of the Edinburgh Opera House Model, which cost £12,000 to build to a scale of one eigth.

Section Three

Now we come to the most important part of the chain—the equipment itself—and nowhere is the concept of a chain more relevant. It is here that items are frequently mismatched: for example the purchase of an expensive microphone can be largely wasted by an unsatisfactory mixer further down the chain.

It is vital that all items are of compatible standard. They must match not only electrically but qualitatively. Often a complete system is too expensive to be purchased at one time and one must resort to a phased programme. This is acceptable, as long as the final goal is still kept in sight and no-one is allowed to call a halt halfway. Frequently this is not explained to ruling committees, whose response often is "what do you want new loudspeakers for—we spent £4000 on a new mixer last year".

In this section we will deal with each piece of equipment in detail, but first let us define our concept of the chain. the chain.

The Microphone

The device, usually cylindrical, is held in the performer's hand (or mounted on a special stand) which picks up the desired sound. It is usually very selective, producing only a small electric current which is in proportion to the fluctuations of the original sound waves. The electrical signal is passed to the **Mixer**.

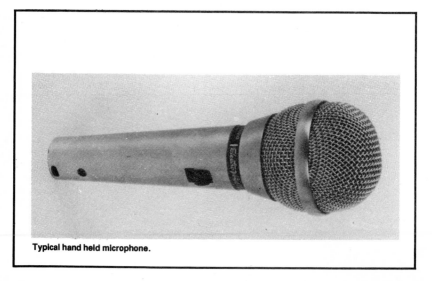

Typical hand held microphone.

Mixer

Here the different input signals are processed, one volume balanced against another volume, and the tone adjusted. Finally, the signals are arranged in groups relevant to either the number of tiers in the theatre, or to parts of the production, before passing to the **Equaliser**.

Sound mixing desk often found in theatre or broadcast work.

Equaliser

This device allows for the adjustment of a large number of frequencies right throughout the audio spectrum. The adjustments are made both to enhance the quality of the sound, perhaps giving it more presence in middle vocal frequencies, and to level out any peaks or troughs created in the system's response to the acoustics of the building. A flatter response will mean more gain or volume before feedback (howlround) occurs. The signal then passes to the **Amplifier**.

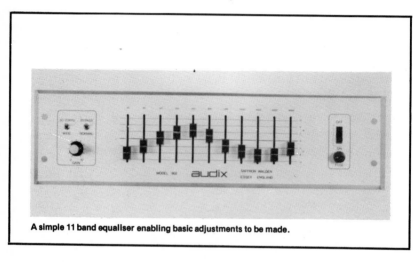

A simple 11 band equaliser enabling basic adjustments to be made.

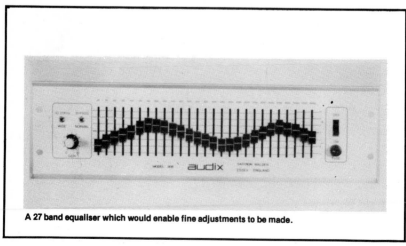

A 27 band equaliser which would enable fine adjustments to be made.

Amplifier

Up to now the signals have been weak, not powerful enough to produce the drive and volume we require later. The amplifier produces this power and passes it along to the last item in the chain.

The Loudspeaker

This unit works in the reverse way to the microphone. The electrical signals cause movement of the loudspeaker cone, which creates sound waves fluctuating in proportion to the original sound.

Such are the basic parts of a system. There are others that we will refer to—delay lines, echo units, compressor limiters, monitors, tape units, disc units and the all-important wiring.

Line source column loudspeakers with covers removed to show the cones or drivers.

Now we will deal with each item in more detail, explain how it works and how it is used.

Microphones

As we have seen earlier, a voice or musical instrument which is making sound by causing strings or chords to vibrate produces waves of compression in the air proportionate to the fluctuations of the original sound. All microphones are fitted with a metal plate, known as a diaphragm, which receives the compression waves and vibrates accordingly.

From here there are two basic ways in which these vibrations may be converted into an electrical signal, and microphones are often referred to by the names of these processes—dynamic or condenser. Note that we are dealing with microphones most suited to theatre working—there are other types using other methods.

Dynamic Moving-Coil

Probably the most common microphone around is the dynamic moving-coil microphone. Here the diaphragm is attached to a coil of wire which moves with it inside a magnet. As it does so, the magnetic lines of force are 'cut' by the coil, inducing an electrical signal proportionate to the vibrations acting on the diaphragm.

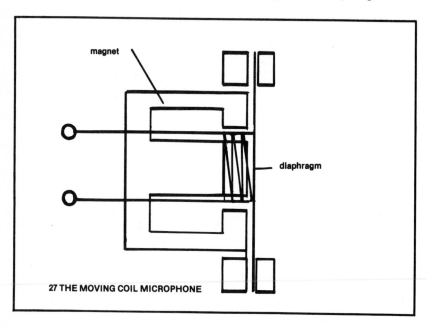

magnet

diaphragm

27 THE MOVING COIL MICROPHONE

These mics are among the oldest types (first appearing in the early 1920's) and are probably the most robust, a point to remember when dealing with some performers—or when mics have to be handed to the audience. A good quality dynamic moving-coil mic will give a good strong signal and can cover a very wide range of frequencies without much deviation.

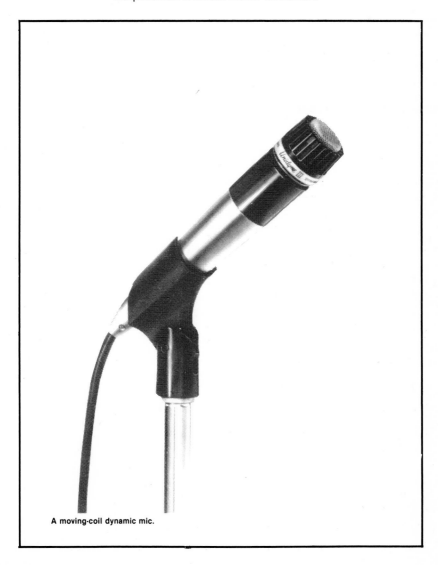

A moving-coil dynamic mic.

Condenser

A condenser, or a capacitor as it is often called, is found in many electronic devices. It has been defined as having the ability of facing conducting-surfaces to store an electric charge. In the condenser mic, one of the facing surfaces is fixed and supplied with a small electric charge. The other surface is the diaphragm. Movement of the diaphragm by the air waves causes variations in the charge proportionate to the original vibrations. All condenser microphones require a power supply unit to provide the initial charge, unless such a charge is supplied by a power source within the sound mixer and fed down the mic line. This process is known as phantom powering. Although there is some uniformity, not all condenser mics work to the same charge so some careful checking is necessary.

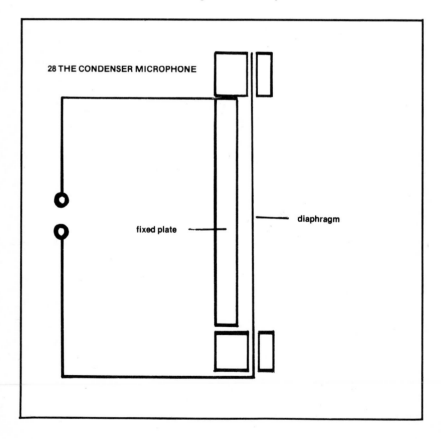

28 THE CONDENSER MICROPHONE

fixed plate

diaphragm

Most condenser microphones produce excellent results. They are very sensitive and have a very flat, even response over the whole audio spectrum. For these reasons they have become a standard in recording and broadcasting.

Pressure And Pressure Gradient Mics, Ribbon Mics

In the pressure operated mic the sound waves act only on the front of the microphone—on one side of the diaphragm. In the pressure gradient mic the waves have access to both sides of the diaphragm. Since this is not possible simultaneously from one source—the waves arriving at the front before they arrive at the rear, various effects are possible and most pressure gradient mics emphasise the bass when used close to the performance. One such microphone occasionally found in theatre is the ribbon mic.

Here a strip of corrugated foil is placed between a magnet and connected to wires. Fluctuations in the movement of the 'ribbon' will induce a current proportionate to the original vibrations.

In practical theatre usage, the terms 'pressure' and 'pressure gradient' are rarely used and microphones are referred to by the catalogue number of the manufacturer.

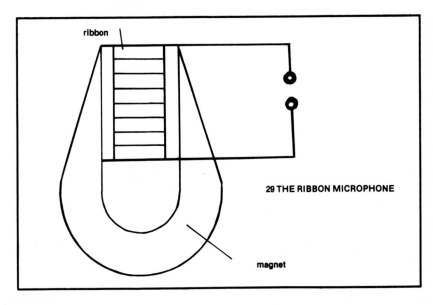

ribbon

29 THE RIBBON MICROPHONE

magnet

Polar Diagram, Pickup, Axis/Off Axis Response

Ideally, we want a microphone to hear only the one source we are concerned with at a particular time. Certainly we do not wish to pick up the loudspeaker sound, or else 'howlround'—often termed feedback—will occur. Neither do we want to pick up extraneous sounds, such as the audience or another performer nearby. The microphone must therefore be selective in its pickup, or unidirectional, and microphones—both dynamic and condenser—can be designed this way. The correct term for this pickup pattern or polar diagram, is cardioid and looks like this.

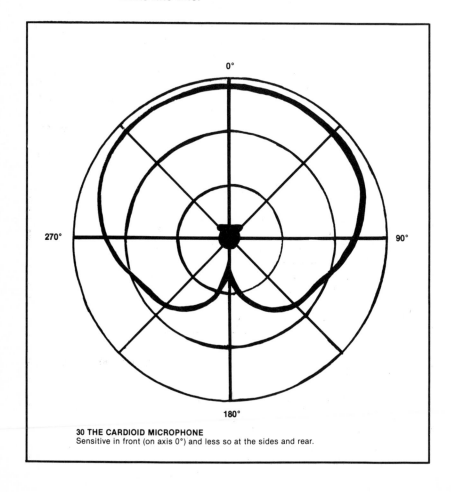

30 THE CARDIOID MICROPHONE
Sensitive in front (on axis 0°) and less so at the sides and rear.

This shows that the mic is very sensitive at the front and progressively less so at the sides and rear. Often mics are more directional—known as 'shotgun', 'rifle' or 'gun' mics, or hypercardioid in which case their polar diagram looks like this.

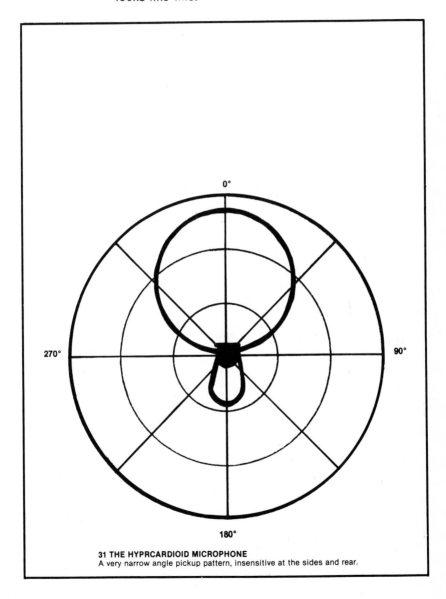

31 THE HYPRCARDIOID MICROPHONE
A very narrow angle pickup pattern, insensitive at the sides and rear.

A microphone that is sensitive on all sides is known as omnidirectional and would have this polar diagram.

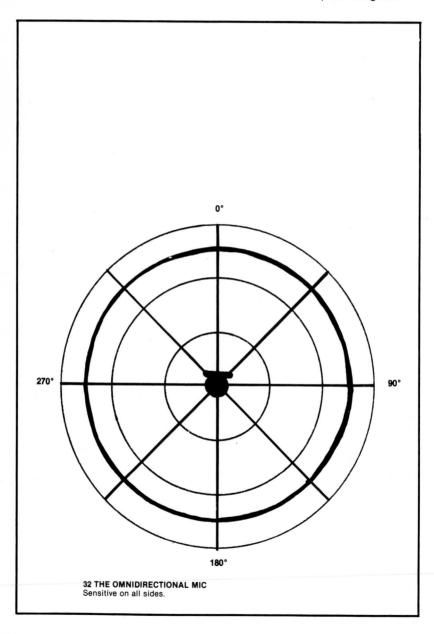

32 THE OMNIDIRECTIONAL MIC
Sensitive on all sides.

Finally the ribbon mic described above is sensitive only on the front and rear of the ribbon, not at the sides.

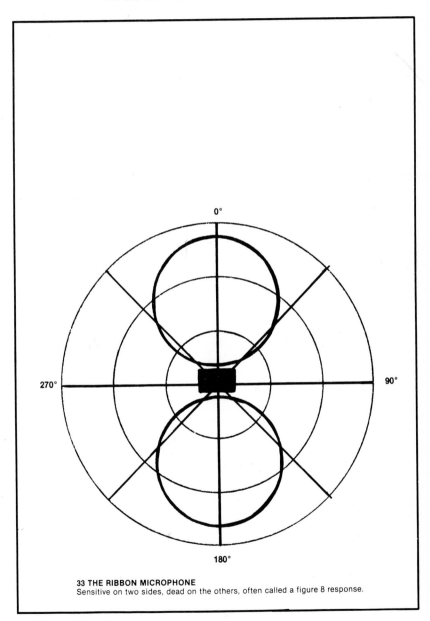

33 THE RIBBON MICROPHONE
Sensitive on two sides, dead on the others, often called a figure 8 response.

All the previous diagrams show very basic polar curves. In fact, the pickup pattern is different for each frequency band, the mics being more directional to higher frequencies. So a diagram produced by the manufacturer might look like this. Each ring represents a 5dB drop in sensitivity.

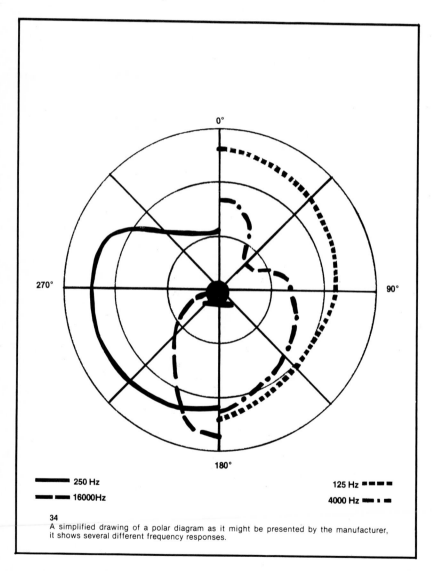

34
A simplified drawing of a polar diagram as it might be presented by the manufacturer, it shows several different frequency responses.

The response and performance of a microphone on its axis (in front) are obviously important, but so are they off axis (at the side). It is here that the microphone hears the sound from loudspeakers and other performers and an awkward sensitivity pattern off-axis can produce many problems, especially howlround, even though the on-axis response is good.

It has been found that frequencies above 1kHz will deteriorate at 90° to the mic, although voice quality does not suffer too much. But musical instruments with harmonics above 5kHz will not sound very bright, therefore the positioning of mics for music is critical.

Quality, Response and Sensitivity

One of the last aspects of microphones to be considered before we discuss usage is sensitivity. How much sound can they pick up? This is often called the output level. All measurements are compared to a reference level, normally 1 volt or 1 milliwatt, and expressed in decibels. Since the amount of signal that the microphone provides is smaller than the reference level, the figure is expressed as a negative. Thus we read of—50dB and—60dB, the lower the number the more sensitive the microphone.

There is an alternative method of expressing sensitivity, which is based on the fact that a normal voice at a distance of 12″ from the mic produces a sound pressure of 1 dyne per cm². This corresponds to air pressure of 1 in microbars. This may now be used as the reference level, so that a high figure is given for a very sensitive microphone—say 5 millivolts per microbar or 5MV/ƱB, and a low figure for a less sensitive mic such as 0.2 millivolts per microbar or 0.2MV/ƱB.

All such measurements are meangingless, unless the appropriate reference level is understood.

The quality of a microphone refers to the frequency response. It is desirable that the control of the tone is solely in the hands of the operator at the sound mixer. We do not want the mic itself to introduce some emphasis or de-emphasis of frequencies on its own. In other words, we require a flat response from the mic.

Generally, condenser mics alone will provide completely flat responses; dynamic mics will provide some boost to upper frequencies. This may not be undesirable since, in a vocal mic, it may help clarity. Some people also like this 'presence' on musical instruments like the violin or harp. A good quality dynamic mic will have a response from 40Hz-16kHz without serious deviation, whereas the condenser frequently is flat 20Hz-20kHz.

Summary

In theatre work we are concerned with selecting the sound source by means of directional or cardioid mics. We are concerned with the frequency response which should be as flat as possible, and with the output or sensitivity which should be as high as possible, measured in decibels where a low figure is good, or in millivolts where a high figure is good. We are also concerned that the mic's pickup-pattern at the side (off-axis) does not induce distortion, dullness or howlround. Generally there are two types of mics, dynamics which are sturdy, and condensers, which are more sensitive and have a flatter response. Condenser mics require a power supp- ·ly.

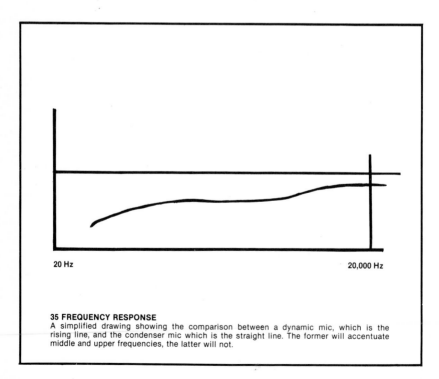

20 Hz   20,000 Hz

35 FREQUENCY RESPONSE
A simplified drawing showing the comparison between a dynamic mic, which is the rising line, and the condenser mic which is the straight line. The former will accentuate middle and upper frequencies, the latter will not.

Usage

Vocals

A directional cardioid mic needs to be pointed towards the source of the sound—the mouth. This somewhat obvious fact is not understood by many experienced performers, and therefore pickup is difficult. It has to be admitted that pointing the mic directly at the mouth is awkward, especially for long periods. It is likely therefore that the unit will be used at an angle, off axis, and the response in this position should be checked. Others use the mic so close that distortion results at high sound levels, some singers producing 120dB or more at these times. Once present, it is expensive to eradicate. Some singers use the mic further away, but still close enough to cause 'blasting' on the explosive consonants—'p', 'b', 't', 's'. Most mics will take an additional component—a breath filter or 'pop gag' to cut out these blasting sounds. It may be either metal or foam and its selection and use should be considered carefully, since some can reduce the sensitivity of the pickup to high frequencies.

Ideally, the mic should be about 6-8″ away in the case of hand mics—further and the mic will pick up the background noise; nearer and distortion may result. Performers and operators need to remember that a mic moved from 8″ to 4″ produces an extra 6dB in level—disturbing to an audience unless corrected. Some performers will move the mic away when about to produce a high level. It is easier for them to effect corrections of this nature than for the sound operator, though he needs to know the work equally well.

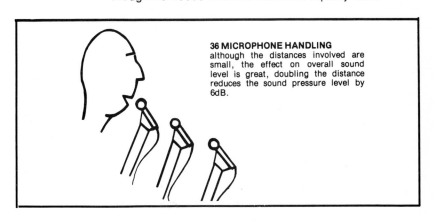

36 MICROPHONE HANDLING although the distances involved are small, the effect on overall sound level is great, doubling the distance reduces the sound pressure level by 6dB.

Sometimes an artist does not hold the mic close, or even point it at this mouth. In these cases, an omnidirectional mic can be used, provided that loudspeakers are not near to cause feedback. Omnidirectional mics can be of exceptional quality and obliviate breath noise and blasting, so they must be considered alongside the cardioids.

Performers are sensitive to mics, and it is often a good idea to try out a selection to find out which produces the best sound and which feels right in the performer's hand. Different acoustics might also require different mics—a fact to remember when on tour, though the chances of a performer making such changes are unlikely.

General Pickup

In most reinforcement applications, we are dealing with the requirement of picking up voices all over the stage and amplifying that picture. This is occasionally the case in drama as actors become more used to working in television and less trained to project their voices, but the major usage would be on musicals, pantomimes and all types of light entertainment.

One technique often incorrectly used is the suspension of mics over the stage. Since much of the voice's clarity is high frequency, and therefore directional, it is unlikely to be picked up in this position. A hanging mic is useful only where information and not quality is important, as in the case of show relay to dressing rooms.

The usual position for general pickup mics is in the footlights trough along the edge of the stage. An odd number is helpful since this means there will be one centre stage—an important acting area. Ideally the mics should be no more than 5' apart otherwise a 'hole' might appear in the response as a performer walks across.

Condenser mics are more popular in this position because they are more sensitive. All mics should be cardioid and some people prefer to use a small gun having a hypercardioid response—more gain before feedback being the aim. Others use an ordinary cardioid and point it at the stage floor where the direct and reflected sounds will not arrive at different times and cancel each other out as they could if the mic was pointed higher at the artist. Condenser float mics are often provided with grey foam rubber mounts, in this format they are known as 'mice'.

The downward pointing technique is only valid, of course, with a reflecting stage surface, and not if carpets are used. Under these circumstances the short gun mic would probably be the most useful.

Float mics cannot really be expected to cover more than the downstage edge, and other units will be needed for centre and upstage. Unless concealment in the set is possible—and this is often overlooked—rifle mics should be aimed at the performers in the same way as lights are aimed. In some circumstances rifle mics do not give a very good response from long distance vocal pickup, and correction at the mixer by means of some added presence is often necessary.

Some sound operators feel that general pickup mics should always be used en masse, so that blanket coverage is maintained. This is clearly nonsense if it is

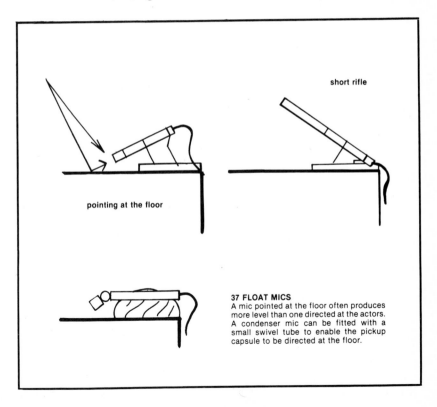

short rifle

pointing at the floor

37 FLOAT MICS
A mic pointed at the floor often produces more level than one directed at the actors. A condenser mic can be fitted with a small swivel tube to enable the pickup capsule to be directed at the floor.

necessary to pick up only one part of the stage. Only the mic serving that part should be used and cross faded to another as the performer moves. Indeed it is important to understand that every time the number of mics in use is doubled, the effective gain of the system has to be reduced by 3dB or else feedback will result. Overall it is important to remember that whilst the stage may be littered with mics, so that every inch is covered, as few as possible should be used at any one time.

We have just mentioned the advantages of pointing mics at the stage floor so that the direct and reflected sounds do not cancel each other out but arrive at the mic at the same time and thus reinforce each other. The pressure zone mic is a new mic which utilises this technique. Basically it consists of a highly sensitive condenser mic mounted on a small plate which collects the reflections. The mic need not be fixed to a surface since it carries its own surface with it, thus it could be mounted on a stand or suspended in the air.

The pressure zone mic, or PZM, as it is known, has a hemispherical pickup pattern and hence this would generally exclude its use from the floats where the pickup would also include orchestra and audience. There may also be other locations too where this is too general. However it is possible to attach a shield which will limit the pick up area. At the time of writing, (1980), these mics are in their infancy in the United States so usage is in something of an experimental stage. Nevertheless users have claimed pickup levels far in excess of any other mic on stage. One particular talent appears to be that of picking up the always difficult upstage areas. Here the mics are either suspended slightly in front and overhead of the relevant area or concealed in the set.

It is interesting that although the basic design of microphones has been based on the same principle for over 100 years it is still possible to discover new variations on that theme.

Musical Instrument Pickup

Firstly, let us remind ourselves that we are talking of pickup for theatre reinforcement—not for recording, where techniques can differ according to the type of music involved. Secondly, let us understand that this section could easily form the subject of a whole book—and indeed some excellent reference is available (see Bibliography), so here we will confine ourselves to general outlines.

It may be considered that musical instruments produce enough level and do not require further amplification. There is some justification for this theory but it overlooks the fact that miking up orchestras is done for control of the mix rather than for volume.

In light entertainment, part of the programme will probably have been popularised by records or television, where sophisticated techniques—often with multitrack tape and several 'takes' cut and mixed together—produce the desired sound. To reproduce this in the theatre is difficult but desirable. The stage may be the performer's market place for his product. Stage musicians rarely have the control of their recording studio counterpart—indeed they are not paid to have—and frequently they change jobs within the life of a production, so some outside cohesive control of the sound is desirable. With each instrument, or section, miked up, the sound operator can blend, correct and shape the sound to that the audience are accustomed to on record. Indeed, with some performers, the theatre sound operator and recording studio engineer are the same person.

This overcomes the problem of poorly paid operation, and it provides control by a person who knows the most about a performer's work. Of course, sometimes in solving some problems this creates others, since the recording engineer might not know about theatre system design or acoustics—he is there to operate the mixer, not design the system.

The rider to this is that most of the sophisticated equipment now in theatre use originated in studios where the larger budgets and greater technical competition provided growth. So some studio engineers are able to work better with this equipment than theatre engineers who did not grow with it.

Musicians do not always appreciate the control provided, and feel that a mic in front of them means that they are not playing loud enough—so they blow harder. It is vital that the whole concept, and the details of miking are discussed with the musicians. They will have their own ideas of the best positions and will often move the mic after the sound engineer has gone. Some musicians express jealously if they are not miked whilst their neighbours are—the answer is sometimes to provide them with one but not use it!

Where musicians are miked up, cardioid or hyper-cardioid microphones should be used. In close proximity the effect would be destroyed if mics picked up generally instead of specifically.

Screens are also desirable to prevent some instruments from 'spreading', notably brass and drums. Since musical instruments generate harmonics going into several thousand hertz, and can have very low fundamentals—a mic with a wide range of frequency response is desirable.

The response should also be flat—any peaks or troughs desired being effected by the operator, not the system. For these reasons—cardioid condensers are desirable but expensive if there are many musicians. A good quality dynamic would be acceptable for most applications—some being produced especially for musical instrument pickup. Manufacturers' literature is usually very helpful on these points.

It is usually desirable to provide one mic to each instrument. This means that drums are treated as separate items: bass, side, cymbals etc., and not provided with one mic as 'drums'. Some understanding of the way in which each instrument produces the sound is desirable and care should be taken both not to pick up mechanical sound and not to impede the movement of the musician.

Amplified instruments can create many problems. It has been suggested that their own sound levels increase as the run of a production extends, upsetting the balance—and other musicians. One problem of much rock music is that part of the sound is created by driving the system hard, producing distortion and overload. This is often achieved alongside high power levels which are undesirable within the context of a totally mixed sound. One answer is to provide a smaller speaker for the guitar—still driven to overload but now without the power—the rest of the amplification being provided by the main system. Sometimes instead of the guitar speaker being provided with a mic, it is possible to take a feed from the guitar amp straight to the mixer—a process known as direct injection. This can provide more control and a cleaner sound, since the other system is open to overload at the mic if the speaker produces high levels.

Here are some generally accepted positions for instrument mics:-

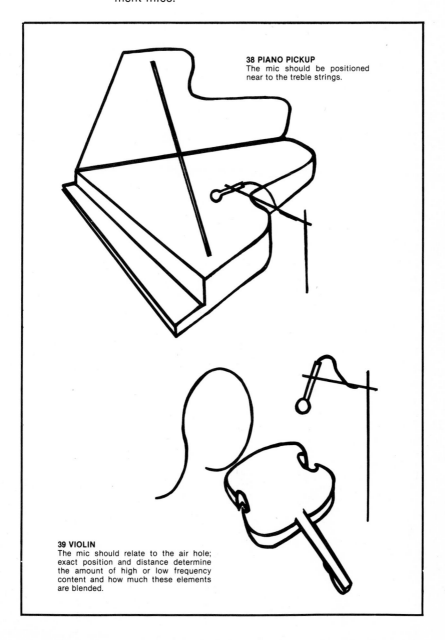

38 PIANO PICKUP
The mic should be positioned near to the treble strings.

39 VIOLIN
The mic should relate to the air hole; exact position and distance determine the amount of high or low frequency content and how much these elements are blended.

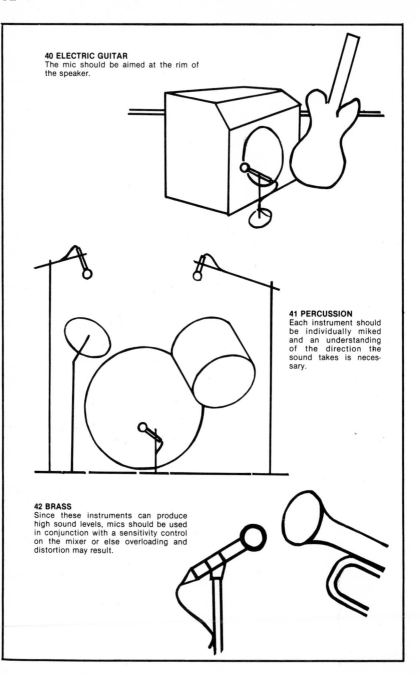

40 ELECTRIC GUITAR
The mic should be aimed at the rim of
the speaker.

41 PERCUSSION
Each instrument should
be individually miked
and an understanding
of the direction the
sound takes is neces-
sary.

42 BRASS
Since these instruments can produce
high sound levels, mics should be used
in conjunction with a sensitivity control
on the mixer or else overloading and
distortion may result.

Radio Microphones

There is often a need for a performer to move freely about the stage and to be provided with a mic, but without the hindrance of the trailing cable. Radio mics, introduced into the theatre in the 1960's, are the answer but they are a complex item and require knowledgeable attention for the best results.

There are two basic types, one a handheld mic which contains its own transmitter, and the other a concealed neck or lavalier mic which works to a pocketsize transmitter concealed on the performer. The latter is used in musicals and pantomimes.

Each transmitter has its own receiver which then feeds the signal into the channel in the normal way. Transmitters require a power supply, either from batteries, which should be checked every show if not changed, or from a built-in power supply which is recharged after each show.

All radio mics are licensed by the Post Office to work within set limits and several mics on at once might effect a reduction in quality. The units can have a tendency to 'drift' away from their allotted frequency and can also pick up other 'radio' traffic nearby—taxis being notorious. In the latter case it may be that some associated cabling—perhaps the earth wire—is the correct length to act as an aerial. Temporary installations are particularly prone to trouble having a tendency to loose wires and bad connections.

Today's radio mics do help to overcome some of these problems by being provided with meters and lights to tell of faulty areas, but they cannot be checked enough.

Ideally a spare transmitter should be kept backstage for each mic in use—

In the case of concealed mics, either suspended round the neck or clipped to clothing, three things are vital:-

1) The material must not generate static electricity— this tends to rule out silk garments. Also clothes with metal supports can cause problems.
2) The aerial lead must be straight and firm—not allowed to bend and break, it is best tape to the skin.
3) The mic itself should be as near to the mouth as possible—most neck mics are omnidirectional and will generate feedback if the gain is really turned up—which it might need to be if the mic is at chest level.

Mics with switches should never be purchased—control should always be with the operator—but in radio mics sometimes a switch is an asset since offstage and dressing room conversation will be picked up by a neck mic which the performer cannot easily unplug and which the operator may have forgotten to fade out.

Now we will pass to the next link in the chain, the sound mixer.

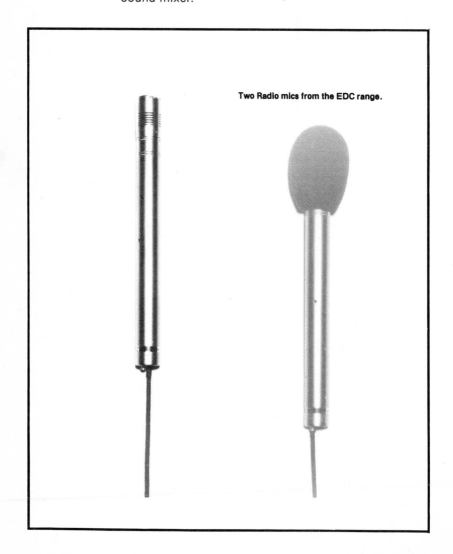

Two Radio mics from the EDC range.

The Mixer

It is at this point in the system that the different inputs are brought together, mixed and sent in groups to the amplifier. It is here that the volume of each input is controlled—and the point at which the tonal quality of each input can be adjusted.

Mixers come in two basic types, one with inputs set for specific purposes—mic, tape, disc etc., and the other with inputs that can accept both mics and other equipment to a certain level. The former are simpler and probably do not have sufficient facilities for our needs, often they have built-in amplifiers.

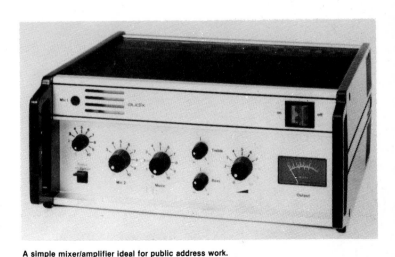

A simple mixer/amplifier ideal for public address work.

Both kinds can be found with controls mounted on a single fascia plate, or where each input section is on a separate frame so that it plugs in and out—these are known as modular mixers and, whilst being more expensive, are the more desirable since maintenance and expansion are easier.

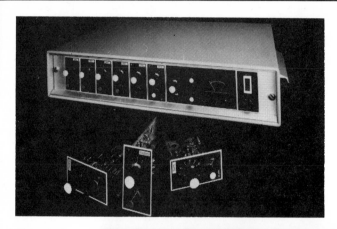

Above a basic modular mixer suitable for simple reinforcement work.

A theatre mixer showing the removal and construction of an input module; this technique allows easy maintenance and expansion.

Now let us look at some of the facilities that are required of a good theatre mixer.

Input—Mic/Line

Having inputs designated for specific uses is restrictive in multi-purpose work—one show might use a lot of mics—the other a lot of tape effects. A good mixer has two inputs per channel that are selectable—one at mic level, the other at an agreed predetermined level known as 'line', which will accept professional tape decks, disc units and indeed most other items such as the output of another mixer—useful if part of the picture needs balancing separately—like the orchestra.

This technique is known as submixing and we will meet it later in more detail.

Gain/Sensitivity/Volume

We have repeatedly seen that a mic can be fed with a larger signal than is desirable—an instrument blowing too hard or a singer using the mic too close. In these situations it is necessary to cut out some of this sound before it reaches the main part of the mixer channel. This is done by providing a sensitivity or coarse gain control, like a volume control, actually on the input to the mixer. Now it is possible to allow into the mixer just the amount of sound we need to play with. The output of the channel is provided with the main volume or gain control, usually a fader and the two are set so that maximum gain at the fader does not produce feedback. Ideally the fader should be able to use all its travel to reach maximum level—the desired level being a point on the scale so that some gain is always in hand. Fader scales are calibrated in points or in decibels.

The sensitivity control affects both mic and line levels though less so in the latter case since the range of power is smaller. A typical specification on a good mixer would be:-

mic input: to match 200 ohm balanced microphone, system gain: —30, —80 dB in 10 dB steps.
line input: 100K ohm
sensitivity: —70 to + 10 in 10 dB steps.

Tone Controls/Equalisation

Each channel is listening to a different source and therefore should have the facility to make tonal corrections to that source without affecting any others. In general, a bass and a separate treble control should be provided and adjustment to boost or cut amounts of each. As a rule on vocal mics the treble will be boosted to add some clarity; the bass cut a little to prevent feedback. The frequency at which both controls operate will be set, usually at 100Hz for the bass and 10kHz for the treble. A good mixer should provide a boost or cut, shown as ± of at least 12dB, 16dB being common on broadcast standard. However, both these frequencies are outside the range of most human fundamentals, so tonal adjustment on vocals is not direct. The provision of a middle or presence control greatly helps. Sometimes this is set at a specific frequency—in which case there may actually be several controls to handle the whole middle band, or else the frequency may be selectable. Again adjustment ± 12dB is desirable. Some mixers only allow for a boost at this point.

To take this further—some mixers provide extra controls so that frequencies of treble, mid and bass may be selected. This is certainly useful—especially where musical instruments are involved. In such a case, it is desirable to be able to effect momentary comparisons with the original sound. Tonal work is known as equalisation, so the appropriate button is called the EQ cut.

The last section of the input channel deals with the routing of the signal. There are three simultaneous routing sections:

1) Auxiliaries/Echo/Foldback

The echo and foldback controls are known as auxiliaries, and can either be set pre the main fader or post the main fader. Sometimes their use is part of the main

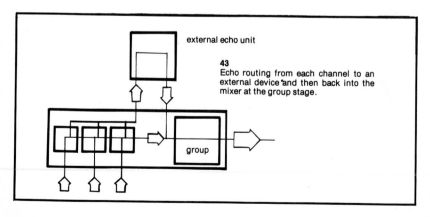

external echo unit

43
Echo routing from each channel to an external device and then back into the mixer at the group stage.

group

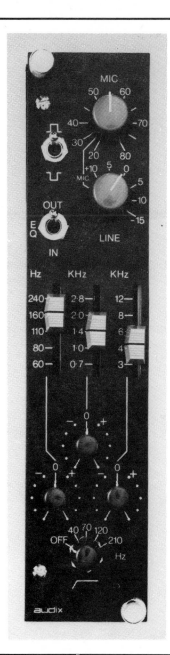

An input module showing controls for input selection, sensitivity and equalisation.

auditorium sound, sometimes not. Echo is desirable on a vocal mic to give it some depth—though it is rarely an actual echo—more of a reverberation and it is provided not within the mixer but from an external device that then feeds the sound back to the main groups again.

Singers and musicians need to hear their contribution clearly over the main sound to judge the quality of their performance. The best way to achieve this is to provide them with a system separate from the main system and which works from this section of the mixer. This system is known as foldback. There may be several systems, vocalist, percussion, lead guitar and strings, each wanting to hear part of their own sound plus others. A recent development has been the radio transmission of these chains of foldback to each musician who is provided with a receiver and a small mixer where he can blend the kind of foldback he alone desires before sending it on to his headset or small adjacent loudspeaker. On some concerts the foldback system is more complex than the main sound system, and frequently louder.

2) Prefade Listen
This valuable little push, often momentary allows the operator to listen to the channel before the audience does, when he opens the fader. It is useful to check that mics are working—such as offstage mics—and especially radio mics.

3) Group Routing
These controls combine different inputs together and send the signals to the main output groups. Usually the groups will reflect some aspect of the show—vocals, orchestra, general, tapes etc., or it could be—vocals left, vocals right, orchestra left, orchestra right, in which case the controls would switch in a stereo balance control known as PAN. Here it is necessary to say a word about stereo in the theatre.

The correct reproduction of a sound picture by recording in stereo is only possible if the listener is the same distance from the speakers as they are from each other. In any other position one speaker would predominate over the other. In theatre terms this would limit the correct effect to a few people centre stalls.

So that in theatre terms we can either use stereo as a simple two-grouping selector in the extreme left or right with outputs not being routed to left and right, but

The routing section of an input channel showing the auxiliaries for echo and foldback and routing with pan to four groups, there is also a main stereo output a/b.

perhaps stalls/circle or stage effects/stalls effects. Or we can broaden this canvas, which would be desirable for stage band set ups, routing the sound of the instruments to the nearest loudspeaker so that visual and aural pictures match. Vocals would be routed to both groups. Float pickup and rifle pickup mics are also often routed to their appropriate side; note that the routing need not be extreme, just a slight emphasis on one side or another.

This pan control does allow for a sound effect—recorded on a mono tape—to be 'panned', that is moved, from one side to the other as it is played. This is obviously useful for all kinds of transportation. A similar effect is achievable with the 'quad pot', a joystick with four corners selectable in different amounts at random. These four could represent the four corners of the theatre so that an effect might appear behind the audience.

In all cases effects should never be so spectacular as to distract the audience from the play.

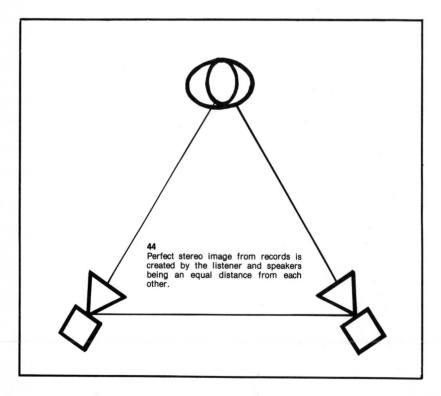

44
Perfect stereo image from records is created by the listener and speakers being an equal distance from each other.

Other Facilities

Phase invert—corrects the wiring of microphones so that they are all in phase and their signals don't cancel each other out. Desirable if people bring their own mics which might be wired differently.

Channel on—just a switch—useful in conference work where a mic might be set at a predetermined level and switched on and off at will.

Insert—very useful to add extra facilities to a channel from an external piece of equipment—perhaps more equalisation in the case of a main vocal channel, or some noise reduction in the case of a tape channel.

Overload—an indication of when the channel's overload has been reached (this is determined by the manufacturer). It enables the operator to determine which is the danger channel by eye, rather than by listening which is sometimes hard.

Output Groups—Sub Groups

We have seen that it is possible to route the input signals to any output group—and that this would normally relate to orchestra, general pickup, vocals and so on. Mixers are normally provided with at least two outputs, with most professional systems offering at least four and frequently eight. A larger number provides for greater flexibility.

Each output group is provided with a fader, usually an echo-return volume control and often some tone control. These need careful use since tone control is also possible on the input module and later in the system by a graphic equaliser which compensates for the theatre's acoustics. However, sometimes it is desirable to make overall corrections to a group.

There is no standard set of accepted facilities that should be available at this point; prefade listen, stereo pan and foldback are sometimes found.

Sometimes the groups are actually sub-divisions of two main faders, in which case they are called 'subgroups' handling a 'submix'. If an external submixer was used, its output would be fed into the system at this point. Such a mixer would certainly be required for orchestral work and might not be positioned with the main mixer but with the musicians. This would certainly be the case if the unit was also handling foldback, so that the main mixer still handles vocals and orchestra.

45
SUBMIXERS AND THEIR RELATIONSHIP TO
THE MAIN MIXER

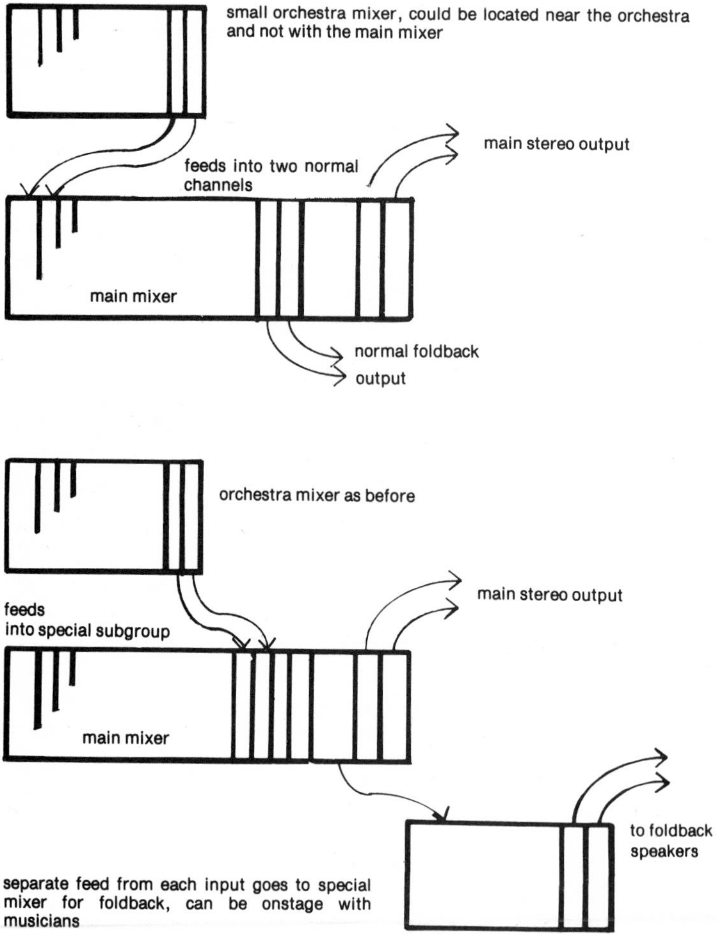

small orchestra mixer, could be located near the orchestra
and not with the main mixer

main stereo output

feeds into two normal
channels

main mixer

normal foldback
output

orchestra mixer as before

main stereo output

feeds
into special subgroup

main mixer

separate feed from each input goes to special
mixer for foldback, can be onstage with
musicians

to foldback
speakers

Vu and PPM Meters

Once the sound has reached the group position on the mixer it is necessary to know how loud it will be in the theatre if the group faders are adjusted. An obvious way is by listening and we will look at this technique, called monitoring, in a moment. Another way is to relate the loudness to a meter scale. In fact the scale indicates loudness but is actually based on a measurement of the amount of electrical current flowing through the mixer output.

The meters operate according to two different ballistics, some meters are switchable to both.

The more common Vu (Volume unit) meter is the cheaper of the two and the quicker acting—so it can be difficult to read. It has two scales—one which represents percentage use of the channel (its measurements are often arbitrary), the other representing a decibel scale.

Broadcast and recording authorities prefer the slower PPM (Peak Programme Meter) which is more precise and easier to read in potential overload situations. It has a seven point scale—each point representing 4dB.

In order to effect some balance to the sound, louder or softer, it is necessary to start from some reference point and all meters are provided with such a point on their scale. Some people prefer to use their own reference point above that provided on the scale but they still use the original as a basis. Ideally the in-

The output section of a theatre mixer showing LED meters.

dividual input channels should be set up, with their gain or sensitivity and main fader, so that a particular movement of each fader produces a known response relevant to the original reference point on the scale. A good mixer will provide a tone that can be fed into the system to assist in the correct adjustment relative to the original reference point. On the Vu meter 'O' represents a reading of +4dB above zero level (1 mw into 600 ohms), most of the travel will be between −3 and +3. On the PPM meter the line up is usually on 4 so that a reading of 6 would suggest overload.

The meter may provide its information either on a conventional scale, or by means of coloured light-emitting diodes, LED's. The latter are easier to assimilate in the theatre's usual darkness, especially since they change colour at specific points in the scale. Bargraph and video displays are also available.

The final analysis of course is that the operator must watch the show and use his ears rather than dumbly adhere to a meter setting; the meter is a guide rather than the final arbiter, since the sound level can be heard. In recording, the meter would take precedence which indicates the importance of the reference line-up levels against a known sound.

Monitoring/Listening To The Show

There has been a tendency in the past to position the mixer in a hermetically sealed control room where the operator is forced to rely on loudspeakers for monitoring level and quality. This is not acceptable, since his concern is for the level and quality as perceived by the audience—and to satisfy this concern he must be in the same acoustic as the audience.

Most new systems are now being positioned in the stalls or circle in a small booth—or in a control room with most of the viewing wall removable. In these positions monitoring of items other than the main show will be done on headset. The operator frequently needs to listen to part of the sound, sometimes to an individual channel. In a closed control room this would be achieved on good quality speakers.

One mistake often made in the latter situation is to spend more money on control room monitors than on main speakers. The two should match, otherwise the operator can have no accurate idea what his tonal corrections are doing to the frequency response of the main speakers.

Summary

The mixer is the device which receives all the inputs to the sound system and provides them with a means of being balanced and combined before they pass to the amplifier. The input signals may also be adjusted with respect to their tonal content. A modular mixer enables maintenance to be easily carried out; it also allows for future expansion. Other mixers may be connected to the main mixer to expand the system, this is known as sub-mixing and is especially suited to orchestral mics. The mixer may have several outputs, some of which are for auxiliary purposes such as echo (via an external device) or foldback (so that the artist and orchestra may hear themselves).

98

Choosing The Mixer—The Specification

If we refer yet again to the chain theorem, it is not possible to have one link more important than another, but certainly the mixer link requires careful thought.

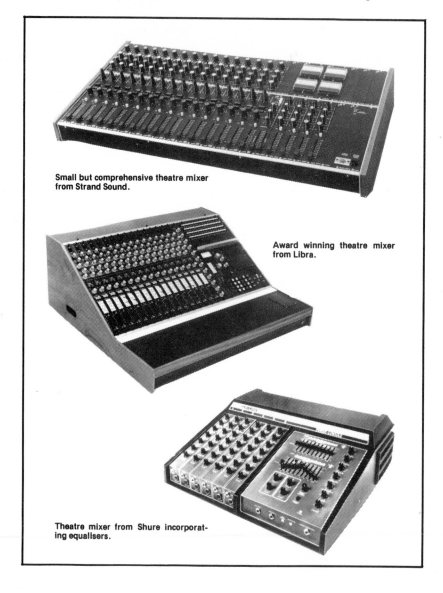

Small but comprehensive theatre mixer from Strand Sound.

Award winning theatre mixer from Libra.

Theatre mixer from Shure incorporating equalisers.

Mixers are very attractive items, almost the only part of the sound system not confining its secrets to a satin anodised box, but bringing them out onto the surface with knobs to twiddle and dials to watch. Care is taken over their shape and appearance, their colour and weight. Mixers are the sexy area of sound equipment.

In this respect it is easy to make the wrong choice; the cosmetic can appeal over the economic and the practical.

To start with, choose a mixer that is modular - this will make maintenance, flexibility and expansion easier than with those mounted on a single fascia. Next, choose a mixer big enough for your needs—then add some. Sound technology has grown incredibly in the last 10 years and doesn't show any signs of slowing down. The number of input channels and output channels should be carefully considered and, if possible, the overall frame big enough to make additions later by taking out the blank module and insert the new channel.

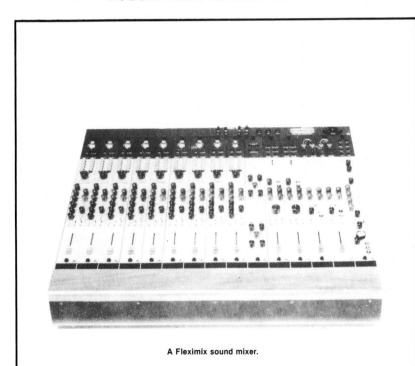

A Fleximix sound mixer.

Consider where the unit is to be used—are the doors wide enough for the desk to be brought in?—an often overlooked fact. What is the lighting like and what colour is it? Can the dials and calibrations be easily seen in such light?

If your sound engineer leaves and the next one works in a different way, will the system be flexible enough to cope with the change—or is it so specialised that only one person can understand it?

These are some of the general questions. The question of the mixer's performance is also important, and one of the most telling aspects is the

Signal To Noise Ratio

Noise is defined as the random movements of electrons within a system, and it can be detected as a hissing or rushing water sound. It is important that this noise does not rise to a disturbing level as the gain of the mixer is turned up. Theatre mixers usually work at very high sound levels and so the system needs to be 'quiet'. A s/n ratio of 70dB would be acceptable for good quality voice reinforcement, but the standard to aim for would be 95-100dB, suitable for a system on very high sound levels. This would exclude most 'public address' type systems from theatre work. It should be remembered that a sound system is installed for a long time and the premise that 'we don't have high sound levels here' is not acceptable since it ignores future possibilities.

Each item in a sound system should have as flat a response as possible over the range 20Hz to 20,000Hz, even if the system's loudspeakers have a narrower response. This is to avoid damaging harmonics that might be reproduced by the speakers from a problem fundamental which is itself outside the range of the loudspeaker.

The manufacturer should also be asked about driving the system hard, how much overload, how much headroom is there in the mixer—how much punishment can it stand. Some manufacturers quote figures for the degree of sound the system will stand with reference to an agreed overload point.

The Equaliser and Filters

We have stated that the acoustics of the auditorium can shape and colour the sound coming from the loudspeakers. Often this is undesirable, since some frequencies can be accentuated, and it is at these points that feedback or howlround will occur first. Even without this possibility it is obviously pointless to provide a good system with flat response only to have some external element then take over and effect its own control.

The answer to these problems is the equaliser. This device is inserted into the chain between mixer and power amplifier and it splits up the audio band into a number of frequencies, each of which may be boosted or cut. The system is usually lined up for a particular acoustic and type of production, then not adjusted till either the production or the acoustic is changed.

First let us look at some terms. The filter is the individual control over a specific frequency, the equaliser is a collection of filters. Each filter may change the sound in several ways—the two most common being the shelving filter, where the amount of change ceases after a pre-determined level, or the bandpass filter, where the response curves towards and away from the selected frequency. A parametric filter or equaliser is one that may change the frequency or rate of attenuation of the alteration. Generally speaking, the bass and treble controls on mixers are set at specific frequencies whereas the mid or presence control may be adjustable over a range of frequencies and so said to be 'parametric'.

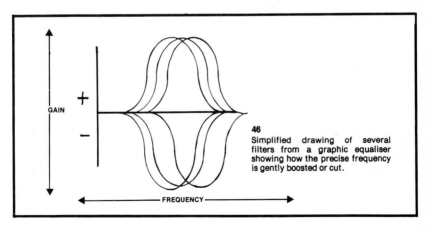

46
Simplified drawing of several filters from a graphic equaliser showing how the precise frequency is gently boosted or cut.

GAIN

+

−

FREQUENCY

The kind of equaliser normally associated with acoustic/system correction is the graphic. On this device each frequency is provided with a slider fader with centre as nil alteration, up for boost and down for cut—the range being at least ± 12dB.

Equalisers have been in use for room correction since the thirties, and over the years the most suitable frequencies have been fixed. In general, filters set at octave levels, that is with a doubling of frequency each time—100Hz, 200Hz, 400Hz, 800Hz and so on—are not ideal for this work since often the problem frequency lies in the gap between the selected points. It has therefore been found that more filters are useful at ⅓ octave spacings—typically 40, 50, 63, 80, 100, 125, 160, 200, 250, 315, 400, 500, 630, 800, 1000, 1250, 1600, 2000, 2500, 3150, 4000, 5000, 6300, 8000, 10,000, 12,500 and 16,000.

The adjustment of such equipment is complex and in the hand of the uninitiated can create more problems than it solves. The equaliser can be set by ear alone but the provision of a device known as a spectrum analyser greatly eases the task. Ideally, equal amounts of all frequencies are fed into the speaker system and picked up by microphones placed on stage and in the auditorium. The analyser then provides a read-out of just how the system and the acoustics have altered the original even input, this is known as the 'house curve'. The graphic equaliser is then adjusted relative to the read out so that peaks and troughs are evened out. Sometimes it is preferable to adjust filters on either side of a problem frequency, even though there may actually be a filter for that frequency. That is because the whole area of the curve is changed this way, and often the reduction in level is less than if a finer correction had been made.

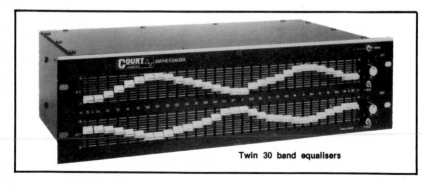

Twin 30 band equalisers

Equalisers can be inserted at any point in the audio chain—they may be connected to a specific piece of equipment, and in complex systems favoured by rock groups, may be found on each item, but generally their use is restricted to the output. Ideally they should be connected to each part of the system that is separately fed—so that stalls left and right loudspeakers in a stereo set-up would need two—one in a mono set-up. If the theatre had other tiers, this pattern would be repeated. The equaliser should also be used on the foldback system—the artist's own stage monitor speaker—though there may be a troublesome frequency that causes feedback mid-way between even the tight bands of the ⅓ octave system. The answer is to provide a 'notch' filter which effects a sharp attenuation at the selected point.

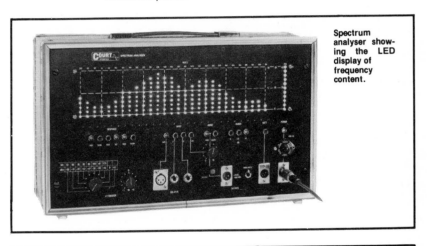

Spectrum analyser showing the LED display of frequency content.

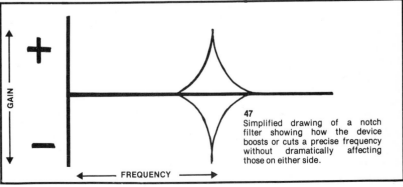

GAIN

FREQUENCY

47
Simplified drawing of a notch filter showing how the device boosts or cuts a precise frequency without dramatically affecting those on either side.

Many people feel that equalisers are a luxury—this is very foolish thinking. Not only do they afford a real chance of cutting down feedback, but also of adjusting the quality of the sound in ways undreamt of by theatre engineers of a few years ago.

Summary
The equaliser is a collection of individual filters which may be adjusted to improve the overall sound. The device usually corrects peaks or troughs in the 'house curve'—the response of a particular acoustic to a particular system.

The Amplifier

Up to now, on its journey from mic or tape, through mixer and equaliser, the sound signal has lacked strength. The amplifier is the next item in the chain and the one which provides the signal with the strength to drive loudspeakers.

Amplifiers need to be carefully selected and carefully designed into the system, because if ever there was a potentially weak link, it is here. The two main problem areas are the possibilities of distortion, or of some fault in the wiring external to the amp which would damage the unit.

Distortion must obviously be kept to a minimum, since the signal must not leave the amp altered in style. Harmonic distortion is possibly the most disturbing, usually affecting the odd numbered harmonics in a way which can produce discordant results unnatural to the ear. Occasionally the amplifier will affect only part of the audio band—perhaps cutting down the bass and making the result 'tinny'. Another kind of distortion is called amplitude distortion—or 'clipping'. This occurs when the unit simply cannot handle the amount of signal being fed to the input. Finally the unit is also prone to noise, which we saw in the mixer was the random movement of electrons in the system.

Amplifier design is a subject for a separate book and so we must make some generalisation for the sake of economy. New ideas are being tried with increasing rapidity, and there are now several professional units which have very low distortion and noise figures, and which are protected against open and short circuits. Typical figures for a good amplifier would be for total harmonic distortion (referred to usually as THD): less than 0.02% at rated output at a frequency of 1kHz, less than 0.03% at rated output 30Hz—20kHz. Two important points here are that the figure should relate to a quoted frequency and to a quoted power output. A distortion figure of above 0.1% would not be desirable in high quality systems. The specification would also quote the frequency response which should be as flat as possible within 20Hz-20kHz, (a deviation of + 3dB would be acceptable over this range). Finally there would also be the noise figure which should be quoted against the rated output. A figure of 80dB is desirable and 100dB excellent.

RMS or PEAK

Now we should look at the main function of the amplifier—the output power. There are two basic types of output—low impedance and constant voltage, and terms associated with these are 'r.m.s.'—root mean square—and 'peak'. RMS is the average output of the system and the figure normally quoted; 'peak', as its name suggests, refers to occasional momentary high points, usually rated at double the rms value. Peak is also often referred to as 'music' power, but we are most interested in what kind of power the amp can deliver for long periods, not for the odd second.

100V Line or Low Impedance

Low impedance refers to the kind of resistance offered to the circuit by the loudspeaker and is measured in ohms. The usual professional loudspeaker is rated at 8 ohms. Constant voltage systems are used as an alternative where more than one speaker is required to be driven from one amplifier. Since transformers are involved there is some loss of frequency response. Therefore these systems (called 100v line in UK, 70v line in US) are usually restricted to paging and to public address. The limiting factor on a 100v line system is that the amp should not be overloaded. A 100w rms 100v amp could feed 100 1w rms 100v speakers, 10 10w rms 100v speakers or 1 100w 100v speaker without problems - all other elements are matched by the transformers, and the cable length and type are relatively unimportant. Without the transformer - the low impedance system gives quality and is therefore the professional standard, but here the entire system external to the amp has to be matched—the length of cable and its size also offering resistance. Long runs from amps to speakers can be expensive, since the cable needs to be thick to offer little resistance. For this reason, low impedance amps are often kept as near as possible to the loudspeakers that they serve, otherwise some loss of power might occur down the line and certainly the cable will be expensive. Constant voltage systems do not have this problem and therefore their amplifiers may be positioned anywhere—usually some remote control room or electrical switch room. Remembering the two basic electrical equations—

$$\text{watts} \quad = \quad \text{volts} \times \text{amps}$$

$$\text{volts} \quad = \quad \text{amps} \times \text{ohms}$$

we can produce a third—

$$\text{volts}^2 = \text{ohms} \times \text{watts}$$

We can therefore see that a system delivering 100w rms to an 8 ohm loudspeaker does so at just over 28 volts, about 3½ amps. If two 8 ohm speakers were connected in series to form a 16 ohm load then there would not be sufficient voltage to drive them, and there would be a consequent loss of power. Conversely, if two 8 ohm units were connected in parallel, forming a 4 ohm load, there would be too much voltage, and distortion would result.

In the constant voltage system the power delivered from each loudspeaker is decided by its inbuilt transformer, and these often have several 'tappings' for different powers, or even a rotary volume control. This is useful since in a multispeaker set-up—fed from one amp—different locations may require different amounts of power, the main volume control dictating the overall balance. It is undesirable to drive an amplifier too hard, and therefore its matched speaker load in watts would perhaps be a half or two-thirds of the power the amplifier can deliver. Most amplifiers have a preset gain control so that **its** output can be regulated accordingly. We shall see in the system design section that it is desirable for several reasons to restrict amplifiers one to each speaker, or speaker group. All such amps should have the same rating, which then makes it easy for one spare to be available for anywhere in the system. This technique prevents overload, allows precise balancing of one part of the theatre against another—and doesn't put all the system's eggs into one basket—failure of one amp loses only part—not the whole—of the system.

A good amplifier should also be designed so that all the potentially troublesome parts can be easily replaced by someone who doesn't understand electronics or possess a soldering iron. All relevant parts should be socketted and the theatre carry spares. The faulty component can then be sent back to the manufacturer for repair.

Finally we should examine how the power output of amplifiers is rated—usually in watts. We have discussed the terms rms and peak, and we know that a watt is a measure of the power available from the product of the voltage and the current. Some specifications alternatively express the gain of the unit in decibels. This figure should state clearly what is being used as the reference point, and whether it is a comparison therefore of power or voltage. A doubling of the voltage supplied is the equivalent of a 6dB increase in voltage and a 3dB increase in power. Suppose that 100w output was achieved from 0.1w input. This would be a ratio of 1000:1 or 10^3:1 which is 30dB of gain on power, 60dB of gain on voltage. A professional power amplifier will express different powers into different loads, thus 340w rms into 4 ohm, 210w rms into 8 ohms, and 110w rms into 16 ohms. It would be usual to utilise the 8 ohm figure if the relationship of amp/speaker was the normal one to one.

Summary

The power amplifier accepts signals from the mixer and amplifies them sufficiently to drive the loudspeaker. It should be selected with particular reference to the amount of noise present in the system and to the amount of signal it is required to produce from a given input. Its output is measured in average terms—rms— and can either be matched to a constant voltage system which is suitable to public address where several speakers are involved, or to a low impedance system where each amp would normally serve one speaker.

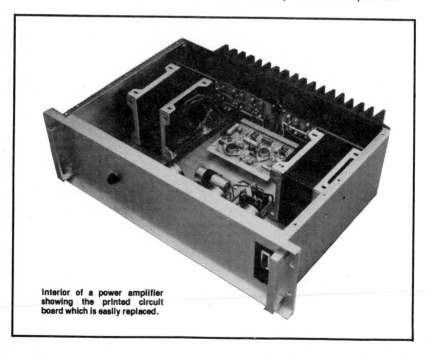

Interior of a power amplifier showing the printed circuit board which is easily replaced.

Changing the Sound

Before we come to the loudspeaker as the last link in our chain, let us examine other pieces of equipment which are used to control the sound in some way, and which may be inserted into the chain between mixer and loudspeaker.

Frequency Shift—Feedback Correction

We have stated that howlround, more commonly called feedback, will occur at a specific gain setting on any system. Some reduction can be effected by the cutting of bass response, and by using directional mics and speakers, so that the sound path is not so direct. However at such times both input and output sound waves are in perfect sympathy—they are in phase. A frequency shifter adjusts the output by 5Hz so that the two are out of phase. In a room that is fairly 'dead'—i.e. one with a low reverberation time—up to 6 dB extra gain is possible. The shift however can disrupt the relation of direct musical harmonics to those of amplified musical harmonics, and therefore these devices should be restricted to vocal mics only.

Another device found useful is the phase inverter, which, as its name suggests, inverts the polarity of the voltage applied to the loudspeaker—this it does in pulses, keeping the escalation of feedback down. This device is credited with 4dB improvement in gain under normal conditions.

Generally speaking, these devices are extra items, added on to the main system. Some equipment produced in the United States, however, has these devices built in.

Limiters and Compressors

The job of the mixer and its operator is to balance the levels of the sounds arriving at the input. Some levels may be very low and require lifting, others may be high and require holding down. Limiters and compressors help the operator to keep control over the extremes of the levels, compressors holding up the bottom, low levels, and limiters keeping down the high. Some devices have both functions contained in the same case and the controls are adjusted accordingly.

Assume that a mix has a range of sound levels of 60dB which might be too much, and that 30dB is the more desirable range. The compressor would raise the—60dB sounds by 30dB, the—40dB sounds by 20dB and the—20dB sounds by 10dB; in each case the compression is half its original value—a ratio of 2:1. The limiter would leave the sound unaltered until the levels were reaching maximum, and would then reduce them to a determined level. In this case the part of the sound affected is only that at the very peak—say within 3dB of maximum, a ratio of 20: 1 over a range of 60dB. The section of the sound that we are looking at eventually, having controlled it - is called the threshold, and it is selectable, as is the rate of decay - that is the length of time the device holds the sound in its control before it dies away. A setting of about half a second is customary for vocal work.

These devices need to be of very good quality or else they will introduce much noise and distortion into the system. They should also be used with care, since in the wrong hands they can create more problems than they solve. These devices find much work in the field of pop music where very high levels are common—where the likelihood of overload is high and limiting is valuable. At the same time some compression would lift quieter sounds so that they may compete more fairly. These devices are applied to individual items or sections and not singly to the whole mix. Some mixers provide limiter/compressors in each input channel or subgroup channel.

Expander/Noise Gate

The expander or noise gate, allows sound to pass into the system once a predetermined level has been reached.

This means that a mic is only live when a direct sound—vocal or instrumental—is applied to it, so that it does not add extraneous noise to the mix. A higher system gain is often the result, since we remember that the overall gain decreases 3dB every time the number of mics in use doubles. These devices may be set to switch in quickly or slowly, known as the 'attack' time, and to die away quickly or slowly, known as the 'decay' time. The shape of the resultant sound is the 'envelope'. These units are again found most often in pop music and can vastly shape the sound that we hear—a fast attack time on drums giving a very crisp sharp sound, for example.

Time Delay Systems

We have already indicated that in a large auditorium, the amplified sound may arrive at the listener before the direct, unamplified sound. It has been found that if the difference in arrival times is greater than 35ms, then the result will be blurred—a loss to the intelligibility—and if the times differ by more than 100ms then there will be a distinct echo. The answer therefore is to effect an electronic delay to the signal of the amplified system.

Dr. Haas found that the listener related the direction of the source to that of the sound which arrived first. The delay therefore is usually arranged so that the amplified sound arrives after the direct sound, so focussing attention on the real source. This is now called the Haas effect.

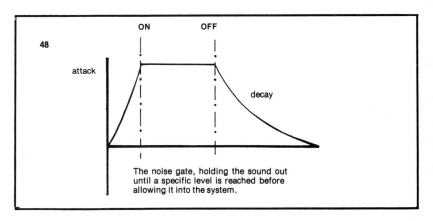

48

The noise gate, holding the sound out until a specific level is reached before allowing it into the system.

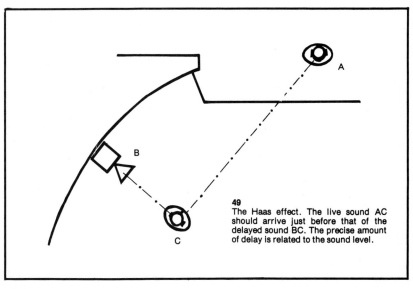

49
The Haas effect. The live sound AC should arrive just before that of the delayed sound BC. The precise amount of delay is related to the sound level.

Ideally the listener should be unaware of the amplificaton system but it has been found that even if the amplified sound level is several times that of the direct sound, provided that the direct sound arrives first the listener will not suffer problems of identifying the source. In a large auditorium it may be necessary to have several sets of time delay systems because the time difference between speaker B and speaker C might not fall within 35ms.

On plan, the calculations are fairly straightforward if we remember that the speed of sound in air at a temperature of 14°c is 1115' (340M) per second, rising or falling 2ft per second for each degree centigrade change. Thus a time of 35ms represents a distance of just under 40' at this temperature. Hence the differences in the lengths of sound paths from listener to speaker and live source should be within 40'. Above that and the introduction of time delay systems would be desirable.

The delay unit is positioned before the amplifier in the chain. Its use can be expensive since the cost is not related solely to the provision of the unit itself, but to the extra provision of amplifiers for a system that might without delay have been simpler and handled by fewer units.

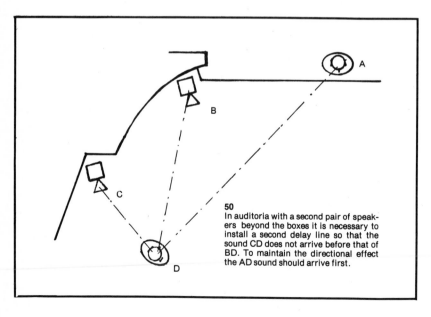

50
In auditoria with a second pair of speakers beyond the boxes it is necessary to install a second delay line so that the sound CD does not arrive before that of BD. To maintain the directional effect the AD sound should arrive first.

Echo Devices

We have seen that the mixer often possesses an auxiliary control on each input channel, to route a selected amount of that channel to an external echo unit, before the whole is returned to the mix at the group channel. There is a distinction between a reverberation unit and an echo unit. The reverberation unit extends the depth of the last syllable in each word whereas the echo unit causes the whole word to be repeated.

Used carefully, these devices can add depth to vocal mix, especially in a non-reverberant auditorium. The advantage is that the amount of echo is decided by the operator not by the acoustic.

In most musical presentations some slight reverberation is desirable, and is only noticed by its sudden absence if turned off.

Most units designed to produce reverberation are expensive—especially since they tend to be stereo so that they may be used in recording. However recent developments in electronics have produced a whole family of "tricks boxes", as they are familiarly known. Reverb is only one of the effects at the disposal of these devices.

They are more commonly found in recording studios and in pop groups.

It is possible to produce some reverberation by feeding the sound into a lively room, i.e. a cloakroom and picking up the resultant direct and reflected sounds by a mic at the other end. In a suitable room this is quite an acceptable effect, but the neighbourhood has to be kept quiet or else embarrassing events like the sound of a flushing toilet can be relayed to the audience.

LOUDSPEAKERS

There is perhaps no other area of sound equipment which causes as much controversy as that of the loudspeaker. The problem stems more from the location rather than from the unit itself, simply because many people are ignorant of the fact that a loudspeaker possesses a specific 'beam'; a known pattern of horizontal and vertical angles of the radiation of sound. It requires careful positioning and aiming in the same way that a spotlight does. In the next section we shall deal in more detail with positioning loudspeakers but first let us look at the way loudspeakers work and at the difference kinds.

The loudspeaker is at the opposite end of the chain from the microphone and it works in the opposite way—taking electrical signals and generating movement from them which is proportional to the signal frequency in the first place. Initially we will discuss the design of moving coil speakers.

There are essentially two sections which make up the loudspeaker—the unit itself—often called the **cone** or **driver**, and the cabinet or **baffle.** The driver consists of a magnet which is specially shaped to concentrate the field at the suspension point of a coil of wire which is in turn connected to the sound system. The actual cone itself is then mounted onto the coil so that it moves backwards and forwards as the magnetic field

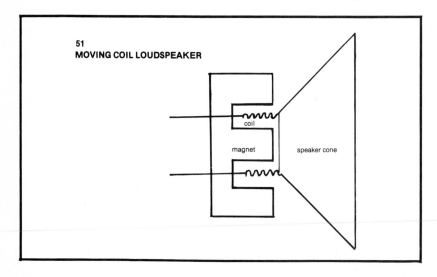

51
MOVING COIL LOUDSPEAKER

coil

magnet   speaker cone

generated by the signal interacts with that of the main magnet.

It is not often appreciated that a single cone cannot be expected to accurately produce the whole range of sounds. The solution to this problem is to utilise several cones of differing diameters, each dealing with a different part of the audio band. There would usually be at least two - one for the bass (**woofer**, LF driver or bass driver) and one for the treble (**tweeter** or HF driver). In these cases a **crossover** is needed to split the signal so that the bass and treble are routed correctly. Some crossovers are contained within the loudspeaker cabinet, others are external and useful when separate HF and LF units are involved. It is possible, and indeed desirable, to add another unit with its crossover for the middle frequencies. Crossovers can be either set at a fixed frequency (passive) or offer a variety of alternatives (active). The latter is very useful especially if equalisers are not available.

From here it can be seen that containing two or three elements within one cabinet is simpler and requires only one amplifier drive them where the same two or three elements assembled separately might require one amplifier per unit. This is obviously more expensive but does permit the volume of bass and treble to be balanced. The sound is clearer—less distorted, if the crossover precedes the amplifier. This is a process known as **biamplification**.

Generally the diameter of speaker cones will go from 18″ to 3″ with 12″—6″ being the most common range. Crossover frequencies are normally at 300—500Hz for

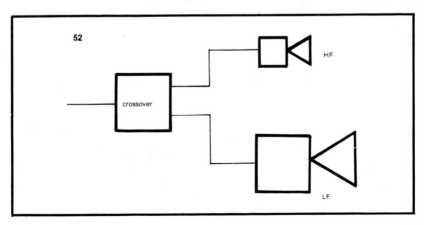

52

HF

crossover

LF

bass/treble, with another about 100Hz for higher treble creating a mid band of about 300/500Hz to 1000Hz.

It should be recalled that the function of the speakers we are discussing is to produce a good wide range; a music speaker of exceptional quality would possess units of extremes of diameters mentioned above; a speaker cone 18″ diameter can go down to 15Hz and even one 12″ can go down to 40Hz. Alternatively a system for restricted use—say speech only, could be quite acceptable from 4″ diameter cones which go down to 100 Hz.

However the performance of a loudspeaker cannot be judged by that of the cone alone since its housing can emphasise or de-emphasise much of the sound. The problem is most apparent at the low frequencies where the long wavelengths can bend round the cone and cancel each other out. The resultant sound is lacking in bass. The cone cannot be mounted on a board or baffle alone, since the wavelengths of extreme low frequencies are so large—22′—that they would still bend round the ends unless the baffle was more than 22′ long!

The cones are therefore enclosed in cabinets which should be heavily absorbent inside, otherwise an opposite problem is created—too much bass. This is caused by the resonance—sympathetic vibrations—of the air inside the cabinet. Most professional units have vented cabinets which are carefully designed so that the sound from the interior emerges in phase with that outside to reinforce it. The design of such enclosures is very much a specialised subject and computers have proved very useful in recent years in calculating how compact an enclosure can be for a given performance.

When it is a high quality device a wide-range unit of this nature is usually known as a **monitor**. This is simply because most units come from recording studio control rooms where absolute fidelity over a wide range is vital. This is an asset but the unit has one drawback which is that its 'beam' is not always suited to theatre working.

We may recall that bass sounds are omnidirectional and that high frequency sounds are unidirectional. In a speaker with bass, mid and treble sections, the bass frequencies would radiate in all directions; the mid would radiate mostly at the front in a 180° angle, and the treble also at the front but progressively less than 180° as the frequency rises. A good manufacturer should quote

Compact monitor. This unit incorporates an HF horn with its own filter.

Wedge foldback monitor for concealment along stage front. The unit has an internal HF filter.

radiation patterns for specific frequencies so that these beams can be drawn on a theatre plan to calculate the best position for the speaker, for example:

Table 7

	Vertical Angle	Horizontal Angle
500Hz	60°	83°
1000Hz	102°	72°
2000Hz	70°	90°
4000Hz	87°	95°
8000Hz	72°	92°

The figures should always be quoted with reference to a specific sound pressure level measured in front of the speaker with a stated power input. Generally the beam angle is taken to be that area within 6dB of the centre beam pressure level. We will look at speaker sound pressure levels later.

The problem with the monitor type of speaker is that the sound can be dispersed indiscriminately so that reflections from side walls can create problems. They also follow the known law that the sound pressure level falls 6dB with every doubling of the distance one moves away, so sound levels set at the rear stalls might be unacceptable nearer the stage. An alternative loudspeaker design—the **line source column speaker**—overcomes these latter two problems to a certain extent. It has another advantage over the box cabinet in that its slim lines often make it easier to conceal.

In the line source column, several cones are mounted

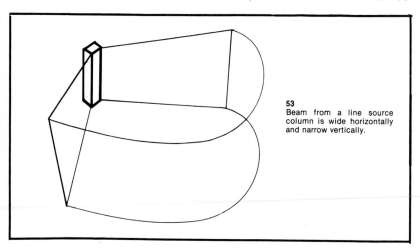

53
Beam from a line source column is wide horizontally and narrow vertically.

vertically and the full power is fed to the centre cone, less to those above and below, then less again and so on.

This produces a very directional beam which makes it ideal for theatre work. The technique is known as **power tapering**.

One problem is that if the high frequencies are produced by all the cones in the column then the resultant beam will be much narrower than those of lower frequencies. For this reason good columns either feed the high frequencies to the centre cones only—or two columns are constructed side by side within the same cabinet, one for high and one for low.

High quality line source column. The individual drivers are also focussed to maintain a narrow vertical beam.

Data for a line source column might look like this . . .

Table 8

	horizontal angle	vertical angle
500Hz	180°	33°
1000Hz	115°	20°
2000Hz	90°	60°
4000Hz	110°	70°
8000Hz	118°	70°

Notice how the beam angle alters with frequency and how useful is the 'wedge of cheese' shape at the lower frequencies.

Generally the sound operator is located at the back of stalls or circle—at least he is further away from the speakers than the audience are. With conventional monitors the sound level near to the unit—say for the front rows—can be much higher than that at the operator—higher to an uncomfortable degree. With line source units this problem is less likely to occur.

The vertical line of speakers sets up a different kind of sound wave to that of the point source speaker, or monitor. This means that an operator can comfortably set levels with columns, at the rear of the house in the knowledge that the front rows are not likely to suffer from much higher levels.

Line source columns came into much disrepute, as their design did not reflect the benefits of narrower beam with high frequency, the power tapering for better directivity, or the desirability of separating bass and high frequency units. The result was that these units were associated with cheap public address, which they were often unsuited for as well. However in recent years, mainly as a result of importation from the United States (where speaker design is taken more seriously than in the UK, with consequent benefits) some very good quality units are now on the market and this design is finding favour once more.

So far we have discussed moving coil loudspeakers—that is to say moving coil drivers in cabinet, monitor and column units. A universal problem with the coil is that it requires considerable movement in high frequency drivers to produce much volume—it is inefficient in terms of translating electrical energy into sound. For this reason, many high frequency units are damaged by being asked to produce more sound than they are capable of This danger is common with rock oriented music, where high sound levels and frequent changes of pure tones can generate so much movement to the extremes of a coil's limits that it burns out or deforms, with consequent loss of quality. Some professional speakers possess circuits which protect the cones from abuse—particularly at the higher frequencies. Nevertheless this particular problem apart, we must consider the moving coil inefficient at the higher frequencies and turn our attention to the horn speaker. Here a small metal cone is attached to the coil. The diameter of the cone increases to a point known as the **mouth,** where it directs the energy into a **horn.** The compressed volume of air quickly and efficiently reacts to the movement of the coil and hence to the original signal.

Bass response is dependent upon the length of the horn itself, and remembering the 22' baffle, we will see that horns are sensibly restricted to middle and high frequencies. Their great advantages are the high efficiency, little fall-off of sound with distance, and precise directability.

They are available with either circular or rectangular horns. It is the latter which is most suited to theatre working, since this gives the horizontal and vertical beam we require. A circular horn gives a conical beam which might have too wide a vertical angle, and this

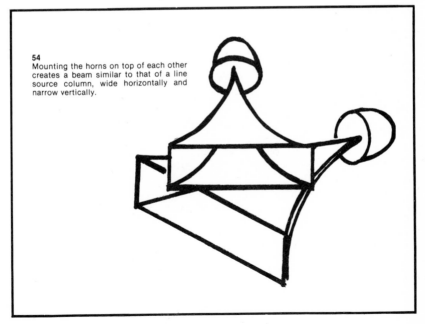

54
Mounting the horns on top of each other creates a beam similar to that of a line source column, wide horizontally and narrow vertically.

could produce unwanted reflections. The horns are also provided with a variety of beam shaping devices, **vanes**, (these are often called **lenses**) which can limit the upper part of the throw and concentrate more sound down onto the audience. Radial, multicell or sectoral horns give a variety of different beam angels. Multicells are better than radials for good dispersion over a wide frequency range. They are especially useful in mid frequencies.

Since the horn operates only at middle and high frequencies, speaker systems utilise a combination of conventional moving coil speakers for the bass, with horns for the rest of the sound spectrum. Removed of the necessity of providing a speaker which handles both bass and treble—the bass end can now be fully developed with cabinets specially designed for these frequencies alone.

Bass units, often called **Bass Bins**, would normally operate up to 500Hz or 300Hz. The point is critical and depends very much on the unit selected. Mid frequencies would be handled by the multicell horn up to about 10kHz although some HF horns could take over at 5khz.

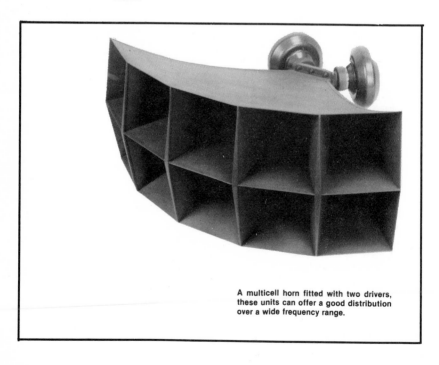

A multicell horn fitted with two drivers, these units can offer a good distribution over a wide frequency range.

So that a wide range system might look like this:

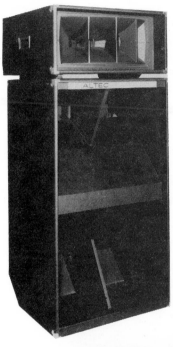

High quality bass unit with separate treble (HF) horn.

Separate bass and HF units. The two sections need not be placed together.

or this, if more money is available:

A sophisticated speaker 'Stack' containing bass bins, mid range units and HF units. Note the vanes or Lens for focussing the HF beams down to the audience.

Although we will discuss locations later, it is important to realise that the different units, LF, mid and HF need not be kept together—often the horns are separated and placed where the directional effect can be better maintained, such as over the centre of the proscenium. On other occasions the units are kept together but reinforced by extra mid and HF horns over the centre pros arch.

The benefits of the vertical line of cones found in line source columns, directional beam and little sound pressure fall-off, can be produced from bass bins and HF units if they are also mounted in column format with some power tapering applied. Vertical assemblies of these units are known as **speaker stacks**.

There is another design of speaker which incorporates the elements we have discussed so far—namely a conventional moving coil bass unit and horn for the higher frequencies—all assembled within one cabinet. The advantage of this technique is that the best units for each frequency band are assembled in as compact a way as possible.

Some monitor speakers are designed this way, and are better than those mentioned earlier for theatre work since the HF horn can handle high power and provide a better beam angle. Column speakers can also be provided with mini-horns to take over from the line of bass/middle cones.

We saw earlier that although the basic design principle of microphones had remained unchanged for over 100 years, this did not prevent new ideas from being tried

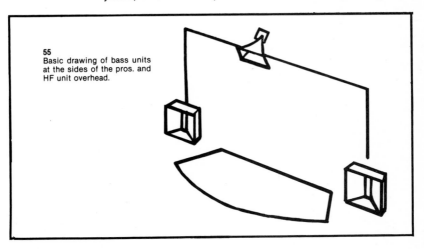

55
Basic drawing of bass units at the sides of the pros. and HF unit overhead.

out. One result was the pressure zone mic. In a similar way people have been experimenting with the design of loudspeakers. One new design is worthy of mention because it follows some of the techniques embodied in the line source and point source units described above. The unit is the Bose 802 and perhaps it should be noted that so far we have avoided mentioning any specific manufacturers: with the Bose speaker this is unavoidable since this design is unique to that company.

Unlike the wide range speakers that we have already seen, the Bose does not use separate drivers for low and high frequencies but employs eight small but wide range drivers instead. In this way crossovers are not required. The eight speaker drivers are mounted in two horizontal rows of four and each vertical pair is slightly angled from its neighbour so that a good horizontal beam is maintained.

Like everything else in a sound system, loudspeakers are very much a matter of personal choice. The particular attraction of this unit is that it packs considerable power at good quality into a very small space. It is therefore becoming increasingly popular in the theatre which eternally requires sound equipment to be unobtrusive. The unit measures only 58cm(23″) wide × 37m(15″) deep × 39cm(16″) high, it is rated at 160 watts rms into 8 ohms. Although the actual driver used is very small, the bass response of the unit is enhanced by specially tuned air ports; the speaker will produce a flat response when used with its own equaliser although of course another equaliser would be needed to even out the acoustics of the room itself.

The Bose is significant in that it is one of the few loudspeakers on the market which is specially designed for the theatre cum concert market; so many of the alternatives being brought from the recording studio or rock world.

We have indicated that some speakers are more efficient than others. Obviously this is a measure of their ability to provide power, and most people are familiar with the measurement in watts as a product of the voltage and the current flowing. Certainly this indicates how powerful an amplifier needs to be to drive such a loudspeaker, but it does not indicate how much power is converted into sound. A more useful figure for comparing speaker performances is that of the **sound pressure** level—SPL. This tells us how much sound is produced at a given distance from the unit—for a given input power. The information is provided in dB in a way that makes it easy to calculate how loud the speaker would be, say, at the back of the theatre, since doubling the distance decreases the SPL by 6dB each time. Measuring speaker-performance in watts rather than dB's of SPL, has been compared to measuring a car's performance by the capacity of the petrol tank rather than by the car's consumption.

The SPL is usually measured fairly near to the speaker—say 3'-4' and with 1 watt input—these figures should be quoted in relevant data; a SPL reading on its own is meaningless. Sometimes another reading is taken at full power, producing a higher SPL. Let us assume that we require a SPL at the back of an auditorium of 80dB, and that this is 64' away from the speaker. Using the 6dB distance double rule we would require a SPL from a speaker of 104dB at 4' with full power. **This simple theory is a guide** but we have seen that line speakers produce less fall-off with distance than point source speakers. We have also seen that the reverberant sound tends to lift sound levels some distance from their source beyond those indicated by the application of the 6dB rule and two speakers would produce a higher level than one—we shall look at this in more detail later. The actual level at the back of the auditorium would therefore be dependant on speaker type, quantity and acoustics. For example in the author's recent experience a line source column gave a SPL of 84 dB at 4' from 1 watt input. When installed the readings from a pair of columns mounted by the side of the pros. and supplied with ⅔ full power were 96 dBA in the front stalls and only 92 dBA in the rear stalls some 40' further back.

Here are some typical figures for various speaker types:

Table 9

	1 watt at 10'	full power at 4'
HF horn (90w)	105 dB	133 dB
column (90w)	88 dB	115 dB
monitor (100w)	97 dB	125 dB

The efficiency of the HF horn is clear from these figures, and it is also clear that all would be suited to the application described above although the HF horn could not be used alone, requiring a bass unit to complete the system. Sadly, it is rare for English speaker manufacturers to quote such data; ideally the SPL should relate to a specific frequency band for more valuable comparisons thus:

Table 10: Sound pressure level of horn speakers
SPL with 1 watt at 1 metre

unit 1	3500Hz-15kHz	± 4dB	101dB
unit 2	3500Hz-15kHz	± 3dB	104dB
unit 3	3500Hz-15kHz	± 2dB	107dB
unit 4	1000Hz-3500Hz	± 3dB	103dB
unit 5	800Hz-3500Hz	± 3dB	105dB

It can be seen from this comparison that unit 3 has the flattest response and the highest output. Choice also rests of course on the beam angle.

For comparison the SPL of the Bose 802 we spoke of earlier is 89 dB, 1 watt, at 1 metre over 40 Hz — 16kHz.

Summary

Let us summarise the facts concerning loudspeakers. Firstly, the performance should be measured in terms of efficiency, measured in dB as the sound pressure level produced at a given distance for a given input. Ideally this should be expressed for different frequencies. The beam of the speaker should also be quoted relevant to a specific SPL and frequency. This information is vital in designing a sound system to accurately predict how loud it needs to be and what is the best position for the speaker.

A single speaker cone is incapable of producing all the desired audio band accurately and therefore there are different sizes for bass, mid and treble, sometimes collected into one cabinet, sometimes mounted separately. Speaker cones can be mounted in line vertically, whence they produce little fall-off of sound pressure level with distance. They also produce distinctly shaped beams which are useful in theatre work. Moving coil speakers are not especially efficient and prone to damage if asked to handle high sound levels at high frequencies. A horn speaker can handle these levels and it is also very efficient and very directional. A good wide range system might have several bass 'bins' with mid and high-frequency horns. Column speakers have been improved recently but would be unable to offer as wide a frequency range as the bass bin/HF horn system. Nevertheless they would be suitable for vocal and background music work. They are especially useful in difficult acoustics and areas where the speakers need to be unobtrusive.

Section Four
Putting it all together

Here we examine the questions that determine how a system is designed, and how the equipment we have just examined fits together.

General Approach

There is often a tendency, when designing a new system, to send for as many brochures as possible and then to assemble the parts like a technical jigsaw puzzle. Nothing could be more dangerous, for this method suggests, by the power of the manufacturers' graphics what kind of system there should be.

Another approach is to ask the resident electrician to obtain quotations for submission to the board. Again this is dangerous; it bases the design on the prejudices of one individual who may be too close to his immediate problems to consider how the theatre is to be used in years to come.

The first step has to be an assessment of what productions are likely to be staged over the potential life of the new system. Since the lifespan could reach ten years, this is a near impossible task. What we do know is that productions are becoming louder and mixers will require more channels.

It is vital that the assessment brief includes all types of events, and establishes which ones are of primary importance. In the 60's many large auditoria were constructed as concert and conference centres, where the system design reflected only the speech needs of the latter function. Once open, the centres' managers quickly realised the potential of Sunday concerts with popular artists, supported by the large seating capacity. They were dismayed to find a system unable to cope with the high sound levels, multi-mic technique and vital foldback requirements of popular music events. The result was that much public money was spent replacing new systems, simply because the original concept of the centres' purpose was too narrow. The brief starts with the requirements of both ends of the chain.

In the United States, system designers demonstrate various sound levels to their potential customers who then write the preferred level into the brief. The system is then geared to producing that level. We have seen how valid it is to talk of sound pressure levels rather than watts. This technique should be more widespread in England. In the case of theatres under construction, simulations can take place in hired auditoria. There are few new theatres that are so unique that simulated tests cannot take place elsewhere to provide at least an approximation of the desired sound level.

It is important to establish right from the start whether the system is required to produce the high sound levels associated with popular music. Herein lies the first dilemma of the system design. Visiting performers may insist on using their own system, usually louder than that of the house, because they feel more secure this way. Generally this upsets theatre managers who dislike the untidy set ups and the sound levels that follow. Theatres often mount their own events and cannot do so without a system. Hiring is expensive, and equipment which produces high levels may not always be affordable if it is urgently required. The wisest selection is the most powerful system. It can always be turned down, but a low powered system cannot be turned up.

Establish a good high sound pressure level in each part of the theatre and make that part of the brief.

Loudspeaker Selection and Position

The next step is to decide what the frequency response of the system should be. It is impossible to work to a cast iron guarantee that music will never be involved and thus the response should be as wide as possible but the acoustics should also be taken into account. Difficult acoustics which are reflective and so liable to cause feedback might dictate a very narrow system in the range 100 Hz—8 kHz. This would be acceptable and, in fact, is one of the ranges chosen by the BBC for a speech only column.

The choice of a wide range system might be limited by the physical size of the speakers rather than by its exact specification. Appearance should never dictate the system but some slight response might be sacrificed, if it means that a smaller speaker could be better concealed.

In large auditoria and in situations where high sound levels are required over a wide range, bass bins and both mid and treble horns are the only real answer. Otherwise monitors with inbuilt horns, perhaps supplemented by other horns, will suffice. Columns are useful if the bulk of other speakers cannot be accommodated but they should always have inbuilt horns; their restricted response should be utilised in difficult acoustics rather than accommodated in good acoustics.

The position of the speakers is likely to cause the greatest controversy. We have seen that the ear can detect vertical changes of sound less successfully than horizontal ones, unless given some clue. This suggests that the ideal position for speakers is to mount them centrally over the pros arch and some of the more successful sound systems in recent years have followed this technique. If necessary, the middle and high frequency units can be positioned here with the bass units—which would be the largest, positioned more conventionally at the sides of the proscenium.

This latter method is some help in overcoming possible obstruction of lighting positions and preventing the units from being too obtrusive.

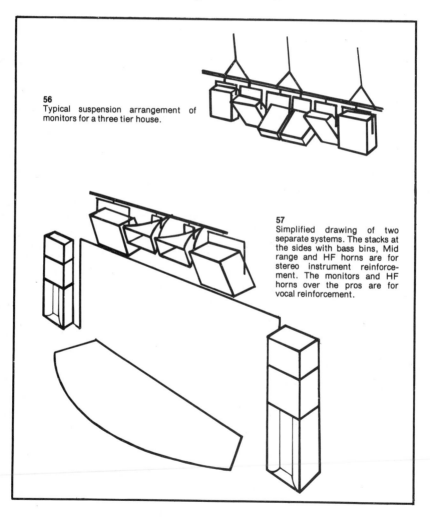

56
Typical suspension arrangement of monitors for a three tier house.

57
Simplified drawing of two separate systems. The stacks at the sides with bass bins, Mid range and HF horns are for stereo instrument reinforcement. The monitors and HF horns over the pros are for vocal reinforcement.

The Theatre Royal Drury Lane showing the loudspeaker positioning for 'Chorus Line', here several monitors are suspended over the pros arch on the right, the best position for good even coverage and maintenance of the voice directional effect (x). Note also the sound mixing position, left dress circle (y). 'Chorus Line' also had rear effect speakers and auditorium delay units.

The sophisticated systems afforded by the pop industry have taken this technique a stage further, by sending the instrument mix to speakers at the sides of the proscenium, where the stereo picture can be maintained, and the vocal mix to speakers over the centre, where they provide some directional drive and cut down delay liability.

This method is certainly worthy of consideration in theatre where there is much use of miked up orchestras. One advantage is that the speakers' response can be better shaped, by equalisers, to suit the needs of that use, whereas if both instruments and vocals are fed to the same speaker, some compromise may have to be forced on the sound in difficult acoustics. Generally it would be the instrument mix that would suffer, with the equalisation cutting down feedback on vocals and adding presence. This latter could more correctly be added, per channel, on the mixer. In which case this should be a requirement written on the mixer brief.

Speaker Positioning

The loudspeakers should always be positioned as close to the performing area as possible—this preserves the directional effect of the artist's voice and cuts down the difference in the distances of the direct sound path and that of the amplified sound. We have seen that a difference of more than 40′ requires an electronic delay. However, a large auditorium would undoubtedly give problems to the system designer since there is likely to be much absorption towards the rear seats, especially in the higher frequencies. The grazing effect also reduces the sound level, as we saw earlier. Another problem is that of the overhanging circle, making it hard for sound waves to reach beneath if units are positioned some distance away. The best solution to this problem area inevitably requires the use of delay systems since speakers require to be closer to the audience for better access.

There are really two positions for these loudspeakers. The conventional approach is for them to be positioned on the side walls further back from the boxes. One problem is that the reduced headroom causes the speaker to obstruct aisles and prevents it from being mounted at an ideal height. The result is that the extreme edges of the seating area are often blasted.

An alternative is to mount several small speakers in the ceiling of the circle overhang. Since these will be delayed so that their sound arrives at the listener after the main sound, the directional effect will still be maintained.

On no account should speakers be positioned some distance from the stage without delay lines, where the difference in amplified and direct sound paths is more than 40'. An increase in volume for the rear seats is little benefit if it reduces intelligibility in the process.

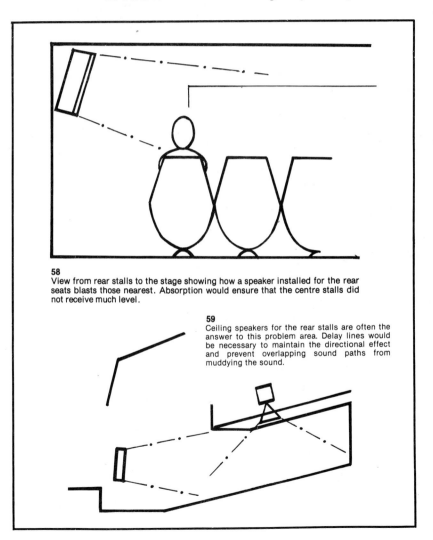

58
View from rear stalls to the stage showing how a speaker installed for the rear seats blasts those nearest. Absorption would ensure that the centre stalls did not receive much level.

59
Ceiling speakers for the rear stalls are often the answer to this problem area. Delay lines would be necessary to maintain the directional effect and prevent overlapping sound paths from muddying the sound.

Let us summarise the approach so far:

General: gentle reinforcement of voice or good high power required.

Specific: what sound pressure level required?

Frequency: narrow band for speech only in difficult acoustics, or wide band in good acoustics, or widest band for music use?

Distances: can the sound adequately reach the rear from the main speaker position or will some delayed system be necessary? If so is it to be sidewall-mounted or concealed in the ceiling?

Mix: what is the function—speech or music, and what priority if both; is there a need for two separate systems—music and speech?

Position: can speakers be mounted over the pros arch or other main acting area without obstructing sight-lines and lighting?

When designing systems it is often assumed that sound levels can be added in the conventional way so that two speakers, each producing say 60dB SPL at 4', will produce 120dB SPL at 4' when used together. This is not the case. Two identical sound pressure levels produced from the same live sound source add 3dB to the overall level. Thus two speakers each producing 60dB will result in an overall level of 63dB. Where two different sound levels are to be added then it is necessary to calculate the result. A table appears in the appendix and it will be seen that the result is negligible.

We have seen that a good loudspeaker manufacturer provides comprehensive information about his product's sound pressure level, for example. The other useful information is the horizontal and vertical beam

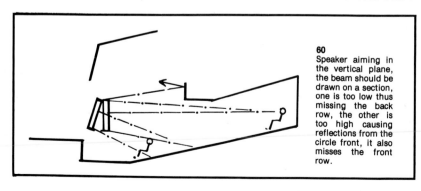

60
Speaker aiming in the vertical plane, the beam should be drawn on a section, one is too low thus missing the back row, the other is too high causing reflections from the circle front, it also misses the front row.

angle. This enables the unit to be positioned accurately since its 'beam' may be drawn on plan and section in the same way that a lighting designer aims his lanterns. This approach is vital to ensure that all the seats are well covered and that none are unduly favoured. It also shows clearly if the unit is able to project its beam under the circle, and where reflections are likely to occur.

The speakers should be positioned high enough to beam over as many people as possible. A high position is also helpful in overcoming excessive sound levels being produced at the nearest seats. On no account should the speaker be aimed so that its beam hits a wall which could cause reflections. This applies particularly to the rear wall.

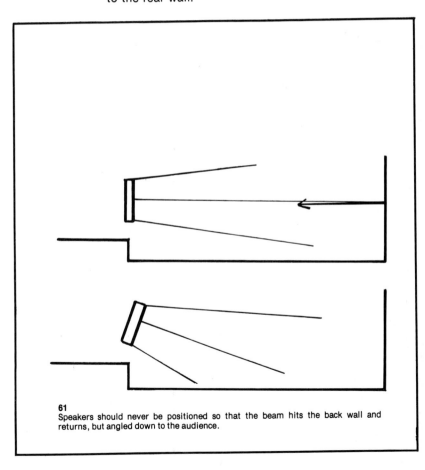

61
Speakers should never be positioned so that the beam hits the back wall and returns, but angled down to the audience.

The aiming of speakers which are positioned at the sides of the proscenium is especially important since the directional effect can easily be lost if the unit is aimed at the nearer rather than at the farther seats.

Generally the unit should be crossed with its opposite, so that the direct and amplified sounds are both coming from roughly the same direction. This might have to be compromised if the unit has such a wide horizontal beam that some overlaps onto the stage mics, causing feedback.

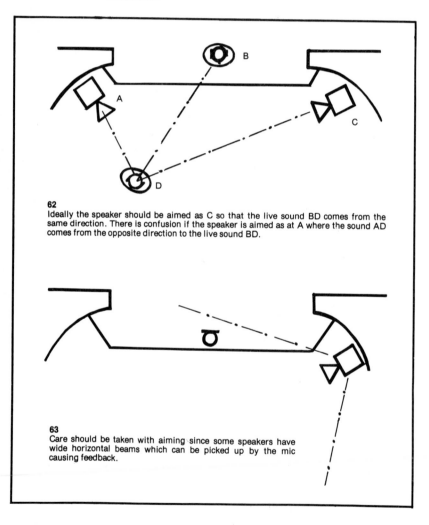

62
Ideally the speaker should be aimed as C so that the live sound BD comes from the same direction. There is confusion if the speaker is aimed as at A where the sound AD comes from the opposite direction to the live sound BD.

63
Care should be taken with aiming since some speakers have wide horizontal beams which can be picked up by the mic causing feedback.

Finally, the question of appearance. Speakers are likely to be installed for a considerable time and it is therefore important that they are unobtrusive. Regrettably some are rejected because they are considered to be too large. The system suffers for the sake of appearances, and the client most certainly is denied true value for his money. All loudspeakers can easily be painted at little extra cost and even the largest unit takes on a more pleasant aspect when it matches the decor. Speaker cloth colour is more difficult since it is usually available only in large quantity, and alteration from a manufacturer's standard can be expensive. It is worth discussing alternative materials with the manufacturer, some cloths or expanded metal grilles are acceptable if they do not impede the high frequency response. In new buildings it is often possible to construct slots in walls and ceilings which are large enough for speaker manoeuvres, and which are covered with speaker cloth so that the slot opening is unobtrusive.

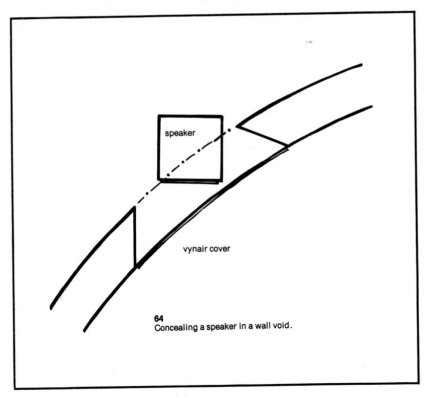

speaker

vynair cover

64
Concealing a speaker in a wall void.

Microphones

One of the important considerations is the number of microphones that is likely to be in use at any one time. This will determine the capacity of the mixer. The assessment brief will have indicated the relationship between vocal and instrumental use, so the general direction of microphone choice will be clear. The obvious aim would be to select a multi-purpose mic for the sake of economy, and this is often necessary. Regrettably the budget often dictates that the choice is limited. If possible the main pickup and vocal mics should be condensers; it will be recalled that these are especially sensitive and produce a good flat response. There is another major advantage in this selection and that is that many condenser systems are modular, and so a small selection of parts can serve many functions.

We have stated that general pickup is achieved by float mics—measure the width of the stage and divide by 5′—this being the optimum spacing. The nearest odd number will be the desired quantity of float mics. This can often be reduced by two if little action takes place in the corners where the scenery is obtrusive.

If the stage is large and action occasionally takes place upstage then several rifle mics would be an advan-

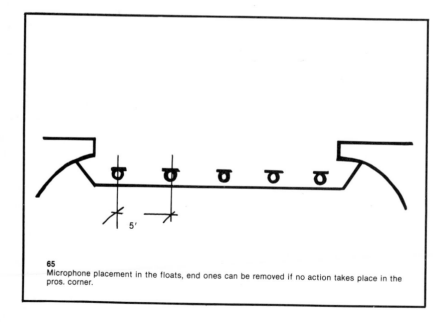

65
Microphone placement in the floats, end ones can be removed if no action takes place in the pros. corner.

Condenser pickup capsules, CK1 is cardioid, CK1S adds a presence lift for vocals or strings, CK2 is omnidirectional and CK5 is cardioid with a pop filter.

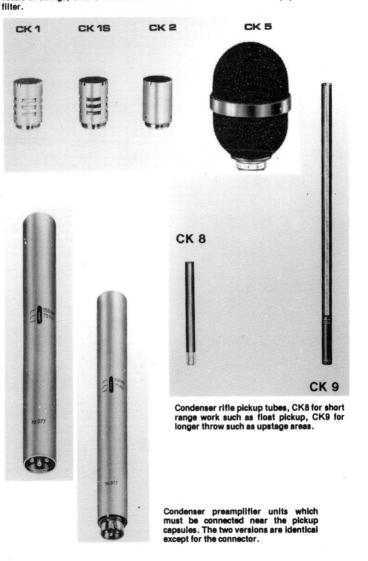

CK 1   CK 1S   CK 2   CK 5

CK 8

CK 9

Condenser rifle pickup tubes, CK8 for short range work such as float pickup, CK9 for longer throw such as upstage areas.

Condenser preamplifier units which must be connected near the pickup capsules. The two versions are identical except for the connector.

tage—for most stages three would be the minimum. In this case condenser mics are better than dynamics which are far less sensitive. They are also expensive so that hiring might be cheaper. The number of relevant control channels needed must still be noted however.

Most stages need at least two hand-mics on long wander leads and these should be purchased even if radio-mics are in use since there will be times when they are needed as standbys.

Orchestral work is also likely on most stages and at least six mics should be provided. Here the choice could revert to dynamics, if the budget is tight, since there are many excellent dynamic mics produced specifically for use with musical instruments.

It may be recalled that the manufacturers' literature is usually most helpful with selection, and musicians will always have their opinion.

The mic selection of past productions will be a useful guide to future trends. The above quantities can only be a guide and each theatre's needs are slightly different. However let us summarise the above.

FLOATS general pickup over 40′ pros.	- 7 condensers with short gun tubes
UPSTAGE general pickup from No. 1 spot bar	- 3 condenser rifle mics
VOCALS	- 4 hand mics on wander leads, condenser or good dynamic
ORCHESTRA	- 6 dynamic as required
	TOTAL 20

Based on this example—the mixer would require at least 20 input channels. Obviously this can be increased or decreased with respect to the exact function—fewer mics and channels for example in speech-only situations.

Having defined the ends of the chain we can now provide the link with the mixer and amplifiers.

The Mixer

Our consideration of the number of microphones in use at any one time will decide the input capacity of the mixer, and the way in which the mix is to be handled will determine the output capacity. Spare ways should be added either at the time of purchase or by plugging in modules at a later date. In the case of the above example the mixer could be 24 ways, thus allowing 4 spare channels which might actually be required for tape or disc. Four outputs would permit the mix to be apportioned orchestra left, orchestra right, main vocals, general pickup.

As far as the channel facilities are concerned it is vital to understand that operators always "grow in" to a system's facilities. They learn with experience, admittedly often bad, what the buttons will do. As the systems and the requirements are becoming more sophisticated, it is folly to shy away from mixers which appear to be considerably more advanced than the existing equipment they replace. Remember that within its useful lifetime its facilities will be considered inadequate!

Therefore consider that there should be at least one foldback channel if cabaret is performed at all; two or more if big bands are frequent, and in this case an echo control is also desirable. The tone controls should include mid as well as bass and treble; more control if vocal work is extensive, either by means of more filters or making them able to select which frequency is desirable. There should be at least four output groups, with the facility to create stereo pictures (for band mixes and sound effects) by means of a pan control. There should be a prefade listen push so that the operator can listen to the channel without the audience hearing. If big shows and loud vocal work is involved, the channels should each have an overload indicator to assist the operator in effecting corrections. The output groups should be provided with both VU and PPM meters to suit a variety of uses and operators and these should be illuminated or preferably LED for the easiest assimilation. All control should be readable in very dark conditions.

Consider whether the mixer is portable and if the access to its location is suitable. Some large mixers will not fit through standard doorways.

Finally choose a mixer which has the highest possible specification; we may recall that the ratio of the signal level to that of the system noise is important, and in the case of big shows the mixer should also provide a good level to the next part of the chain. It would be undesirable to run it flat out and under-running would mean working closer to the noise level. We will discuss the system balance later.

Amplification, from mixer to speaker

We appreciate that the amplifier's function is to drive the loudspeakers; in this respect, one is useless without the other, but we should appreciate that it is the demands of the speaker which are the determining factor in amplifier selection. It is astonishing how often one meets a badly designed system which originated from some bald consideration that 'a couple of 100w amps is more than enough for us—the last system only had one.' No mention is made of how they relate to the speakers.

Obviously the speaker system must be designed first and the mixer use also needs to be known at this point—a consideration of mono or stereo is valuable, of whether the vocal mix is to be fed to speakers separate from those handling the instrument mix. Each different use requires a different amplifier chain. Ideally, each loudspeaker should have its own amplifier for two reasons.

Firstly, it obeys the 'eggs in one basket' rule, if the amp fails only one speaker is affected; one amp serving the entire system would be foolish. Secondly it enables the balance of speaker levels in the auditorium to be easily set. Generally each tier would require a different volume; perhaps front stalls set at a different level from the delay lines further back. Usually once set, the preset level is not changed. A useful tip is to provide an additional preset-gain for each amp on a separate panel— the gain on the amp itself can then be left at full, and there is no rebalancing to take place if the amp is changed.

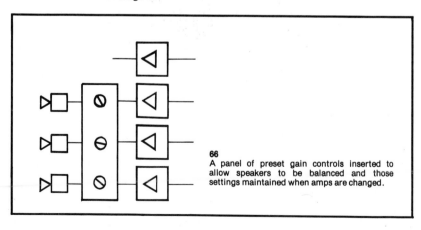

66
A panel of preset gain controls inserted to allow speakers to be balanced and those settings maintained when amps are changed.

An amplifier rack with separate preset
gain panel top left, this enables amps to
be changed without changing settings.

Ideally, all the amps should be rated the same—this means that only one spare needs to be provided for the whole system. Amps of differing powers in a system require several spares, which is expensive. It is also desirable to provide amps rated considerably higher than the speakers they feed, since it is unwise to drive amplifiers too hard. For example, if a speaker required 100w rms to produce the desired sound pressure level it would be unwise to supply this from a 100w power amplifier since it would be required to work flat out. Generally an amp should be utilised to no more than 60% of its capacity, although this is by no means a hard and fast figure. Generally the speakers would not be fully driven either, because this is also undesirable.

So, there would be separate chains of amps for each part of the theatre—front stalls/rear stalls or stalls/circle. These chains would again be divided if stereo was being fed to these areas, or if there were separate mixers for vocals and instruments where each had different speakers. It may be recalled that 100v line amps are not desirable on high quality systems, since the 100v transformer impairs the frequency response. They are acceptable however on restricted band systems—speech only—and amplifiers can be placed at some distance from the speakers because there is no loss of power down the cable. Low impedence amplifiers can suffer from loss of power on long cable runs, and so are usually placed close to the speaker position. It is a mistake to choose a location which is inaccessible during the performance itself so this rules out the apron or boxes as the amplifier position. More suitable are wings, perches or void areas behind the proscenium or the boxes.

Other items are incorporated into the system at this point, notably crossovers, delay lines and equalisers. We may recall that crossovers are more beneficial before the amplifier stage so that the volume of bass, treble and mid can be more easily matched and so that the sound may be 'cleaner'. The number of equalisers will relate to the number of amplifier chains. Again there should be one for the left channel and one for the right channel in a stereo system, with this pattern repeated for each tier of the theatre.

Let us prepare some diagrams of systems from the output of the mixer onwards. We will assume that we are provided with a stereo feed. But first here is an indica-

Sound system built into rack with disc and tape units, modular mixer and amplifier section with selection panel.

tion of the symbols involved. The first drawing shows a simple system with two speakers.

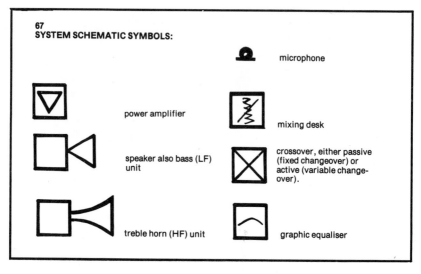

67
SYSTEM SCHEMATIC SYMBOLS:

microphone

power amplifier

speaker also bass (LF) unit

treble horn (HF) unit

mixing desk

crossover, either passive (fixed changeover) or active (variable change-over).

graphic equaliser

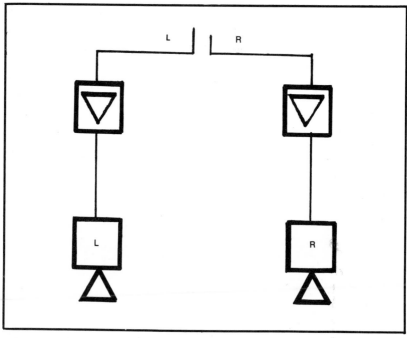

If we wanted to effect some corrections to the sound by adding equalisers then the picture would look like this:

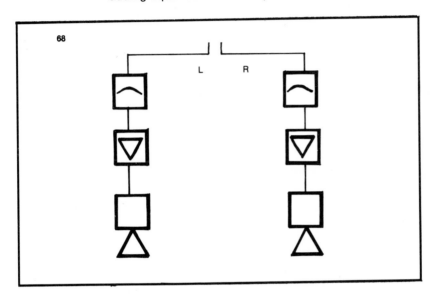

As an alternative, a simple mono system with equaliser would be:

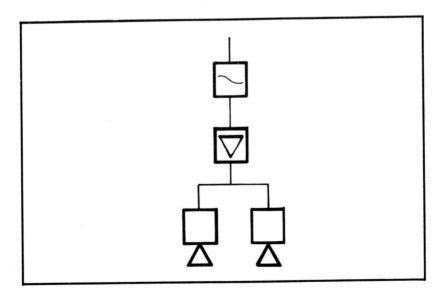

With a duplication for two levels:

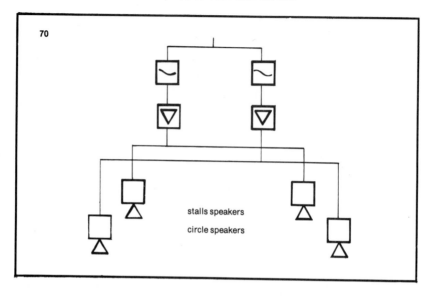

stalls speakers

circle speakers

The substitution of wide range units add some complications, first one level, stereo with bass bins and treble horns:

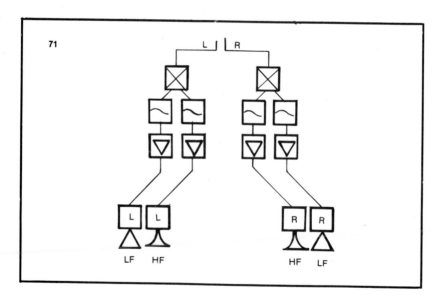

This would now be repeated for each level as below. Let us also now add a central cluster of horns to reinforce the higher frequency content for improved clarity.

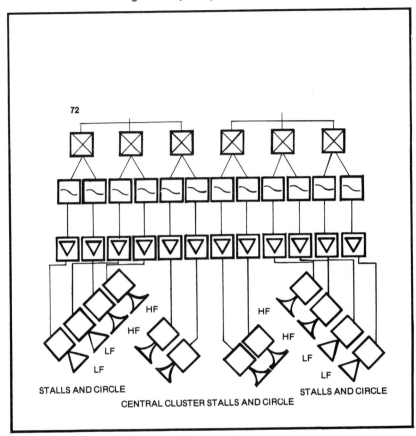

Where the auditorium is so large that mid auditorium speakers are used, then delay lines would be added. Perhaps they would be provided without equalisers for the sake of economy. In fact the last two drawings are lavish in their use of equalisers and economies could be made if variable (active) crossovers were used for flexibility and the equalisers omitted, although room equalisation would not be possible as a result.

Block diagrams of this kind are invaluable in working out how the system is to be used and what quantities of each piece of equipment are required.

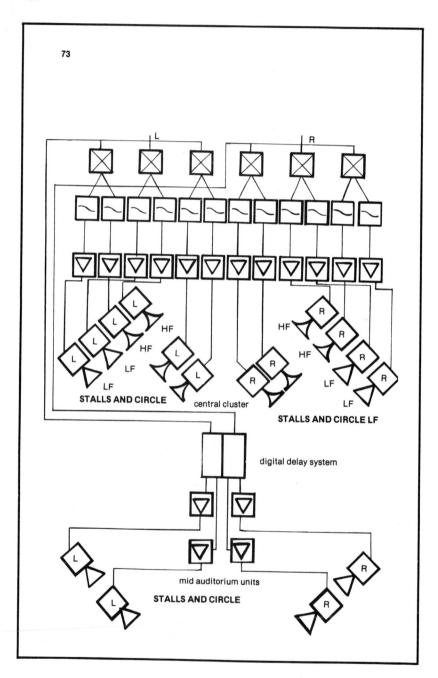

The System Balance

At this point, we should mention the subject of distribution amplifiers. These devices enable a single input—usually at line level—to feed several outputs. A typical use would be where a mixer output channel is required to drive several amplifiers. Normally professional equipment is designed to do so without the need for a distribution amplifier, but sometimes there is some loss of signal where several pieces of equipment like equalisers, delay lines and crossovers intervene and a distribution amplifier can restore this. The device can also act like a fuse and prevent faults from damaging other parts of the system. Finally they are usually provided with preset gain controls so that further balancing is available. Generally speaking the mixer output would be more than capable of driving several amplifiers. The position of this unit is critical since two loss inducing devices should not be placed next to each other in the system or else the noise level will rise. They should therefore be interrupted by the line amplifier unit.

In the United States system design is more sophisticated, and calculations are made of the amount of gain needed to drive the amplifier so that it will produce a certain sound pressure level from the associated speaker. The losses induced by the various components can be calculated and set against the signal strength produced by the mixer. It can then be determined where, and how much, line gain is needed. Sometimes the reverse applies and one stage can feed too much signal to another so that a reduction is needed. This is provided by a device known as **pad** and ideally it should be variable.

In more general terms the system should be assembled to achieve the highest level of signal above the system noise, the lowest distortion and the highest possible safety factor to handle overloads. In this latter respect it is important that all parts of the system reach overload at the same time, otherwise our weak link theory is present again. In the system there should be some spare capacity to handle overload—and occasional peaks; we have already spoken of the desirability of underrunning the power amplifier. This spare capacity is known as **headroom** and all components in the system should have equal amounts. In other words all components should be adjusted so that they all have the same number of dB's in hand before their maximum gain is reached. In modest powered systems—say ordinary vocal and straight reinforcement, 10dB should be sufficient, but on larger shows, especially those with rock or big band potential, much more is needed. Some specially built rock mixers provide more than 30dB headroom above normal operating levels.

To set up a system in this way it is necessary to feed into a microphone channel the normal programme level and then adjust channel sensitivity and gain controls so that the meter shows the desired headroom available. This process is repeated down the chain until the amplifier is reached, where the final programme levels should always be made on the adjacent preset gain control described earlier.

Authentic Reinforcement

The 'black boxes' of equipment that form a sound system frequently appear to have a life of their own: a kind of silent malevolent spirit which withholds its secrets and often refuses to cooperate. Even experienced engineers display a certain amount of relief when a reasonable sound emerges on the first occasion of a system's use!

This perhaps illustrates one of the dangers about the medium. It is possible to become too concerned about the hardware and the sound suffers as a result. Just as a lighting designer must think in terms of pictures rather than of instruments, then so must the sound system designer imagine what he wants to hear from the system in terms of sound level and quality, before he becomes bogged down in the nuts and bolts. He must visit the theatre and visualise what each part of the theatre will sound like. He must also try and picture the relationship of the direct sounds, the actor's voices and orchestra, to those from his sound system.

The most frequent criticism levelled at designers is that their systems generate too much volume. An analysis of such comments can reveal a variety of unsupported claims. Adjacent couples often argue, one felt it was good, the other too loud, whose opinion does the designer listen to? Occasionally the patron disliked the other aspects of the show but found sound the easiest target. Frequently however the complaint is accurate. Only by provided a good operator can we have any chance of avoiding this problem.

There are many reasons for bad operating besides that of plain incompetance. Firstly the system designer has to consider this individual as a part of his overall scheme and hence he must be brought into the design stage. Usually the sound operator is the assistant stage manager who doesn't have many props that week. We have already said that the position of the control is vital. The operator must be in the same acoustic as his audience, if this means that someone else has to do props then so be it. Access to the same acoustic by means of a removable control room window is not quite the same thing. The operator must understand what the controls on his system can do, this might sound obvious but many systems are set up by the designer in rehearsal and the operator is left to balance levels alone. Nor must the operator use the system to show off to his friends, knob twiddles are a great ego booster.

Above all the operator must listen. This is very difficult because by the time that the show is run in he will know the script very well. This means that he may subconsciously think the sound is clear, but this is actually because he knows the words and his brain is providing the missing links from its memory bank. Hence he may not make adjustments that are needed.

The operator must like the design of the system and the show it serves, otherwise he cannot be sympathetic to them and operate with sensitivity.

The sound designer must take all these factors into account. One of his main problems is the preservation of authenticity, making the actor's amplified voice come from the same direction as his actual voice. This problem is the most acute at the front rows since by definition the loudspeakers cannot be located where the audience are looking at the stage. Some conflict is unavoidable for these patrons and it is this location that provides the designer with his most frequent complaints, and his greatest challenge. Many designers live with some degree of problem here for the sake of preserving a greater benefit for those further back.

We have seen how general pickup mics in the footlights can be 'panned' left or right so that their sound emerges from left or right loudspeakers. Ideally the location would not be extreme but would generate an emphasis to direction. However many productions use radio mics concealed on the performer who is moving about the stage. It is clearly nonsense to go to the expense and trouble of providing a hidden source of pickup, in theory so that we will think the actor has a good voice, and at the same time accept that the actor's voice will emerge from just about everywhere in the building except where we are looking.

One way round this problem may be to separate out from the mixing console those items which deal with the balance of the stage picture, the pan controls. These could be operated separately in a way that the actor's voice would move across the picture as he did in reality. This is obviously not easy and calls again for some considerable degree of sensitivity from the operator, particularly in avoiding extremes.

In a more sophisticated system the picture could be broken up into a number of zones across the stage. Each zone would have its own system, so that it would be served by its own float mics and rifle mics, have its own amplifiers etc. and its own speakers. Radio mics would be mixed into that control when the actor walked into that zone.

The system balance would favour the occupied zone with progressively less amounts of level being fed to neighbouring zones. This clearly suggests some assistance for the operator and digital processing may help. Speaker location for such a system is difficult and the most likely place is over the pros. arch. Again the front rows would suffer because the sound would be almost directly over their heads but this has been solved by building a large number of very small speakers into the orchestra rail or stage front. What in fact we have in this system is a linear version of the system described later for theatre in the round use.

The design of sound in the theatre is in its infancy by comparison with the other technical departments. We are accustomed to talking in terms of the design of costumes, scenery and lighting and we imply that the realisation involved a high degree of creativity in the process. Although each of these three fields is highly technical in its own way, we are also accustomed to designers being impractical and having some extra assistance to realise their efforts in concrete forms. By comparison, sound is almost wholly technical, there appears to be no creative aspect at all. In both England and the United States only a mere handful of individuals have brought any kind of artistic interpretation to the reinforcement of voice or the generation of sound effects. Perhaps this is because the medium is intangible and subjective to a high degree. But it must also be because the funds have consistently been denied this branch of theatre, so dreams must remain largely dreams. Another reason is the reluctance of managements to permit sound system designers to locate their equipment in the most desirable part of the theatre.

There are signs that these problems are being overcome, notably on the big West End or Broadway productions which so often introduce new techniques. It is not unknown for other theatres to adopt new ideas once they have been tried, and paid for, by someone else.

With more freedom and more money, the design of sound systems can improve and show us a high degree inventiveness as yet unrealised. It is time to forget the traditional locations and easy solutions and use the building bricks in a new way. The prospects of designer and operator, working together, to produce a high quality and authentic sound are now better than ever before. Above all the designer must try not to repeat a system that he knows works in another location, but must ask himself, 'what am I trying to achieve here?'.

Summary

The system design is based upon the use and relates to the number of input sources and desired sound pressure level. In selecting and positioning loudspeakers the appearance of the auditorium should not be forgotten. Line source column speakers are the most easily concealed but seldom of the highest quality. Wider response systems can sometimes achieve excellent results if suspended centrally over the pros arch. The rear auditorium needs great care if a good level is to be achieved with some maintenance of the directional effect. Ceiling speakers with delay lines are often the answer. Each part of the auditorium has to be treated on its own merits and often the wisest method is to provide it with its own amplifier and equaliser. The whole system should be designed so that all components operate in sympathy, none reaching overload before another.

In describing how we can 'put it all together' we have omitted one link, no more vital than the others unless forgotten, that of the actual installation itself—the plugs, sockets and wiring; the next section deals with these items.

Connections and Cabling

Sound is of course unseen. The cabling and connections of the system are even more unseen by theatre managers. The installation is not glamorous; unlike impressive mixers and control areas it cannot be shown off—indeed it frequently causes the decor to be repainted: it is often untidy.

But it is necessary once more to invoke our weak link theory for two reasons. First, expensive systems rely on small connections, they need to be sturdy and reliable. Second, sound signals are weak by comparison to the strengths of other electrical currents in theatres and prone to interference. A good installation can overcome this.

Balanced Lines

An unbalanced line is that most commonly (but not exclusively) associated with domestic equipment and it consists of a single wire plus a shield which is earthed. The voltage between the two is the signal. This system is prone to a number of problems, notably to interference. For example it is feasible for the shield on one piece of equipment to be earthed in a different way to that on another piece of equipment which is connected by the unbalanced line. The resulting interference is picked up by the earth loop thus created. We will see in a moment how these may be overcome.

A balanced line is that which contains two signal carrying conductors plus a shield. One conductor is positive, the other negative and so any interference effects both parts of the signal and is cancelled out. Most professional equipment follows this practice. It is a mistake however to assume that a balanced line system could not suffer from an earth loop so the connection of the shield is still very important. Some balanced lines are often termed 'floating'. This means that the equipment involved has transformers on either inputs or outputs. The transformers offer still more advantages although they are now being replaced by complex electronic circuitry.

Mic and line level cables should have conductors which are at least 24/0.2mm diameter and they should be enclosed in a braided screen and in metal conduit or trunking. On no account should mic or line level wiring be taken nearer than 200mm (say 8″) to mains cabling. Long parallel runs of mics and mains or speakers are not desirable and they should cross each other only where necessary, and then only at 90°. On no account should mic or line level cabling (or sound equipment in general) be positioned near to main switchgear or other electrical equipment with a potentially strong 'field', or near thyristor lighting.

Earth Loops

All mic and line level cables possess earth or shield conductors and all mains cables from equipment does so. It is possible that this may be inadvertently connected in such a way that an 'earth loop' is created. This will result in much interference from mains and from radio pickup of minicabs, police radio etc. Therefore the earth circuit should be arranged so that it is connected to ground only once with each system or system section as shown in diagram below.

This principle applies to any equipment added to a system for however temporary a period. Temporary wiring of extra mixers or amplifiers could cause problems with earth loops, as could the connection of some test equipment such as oscilloscopes.

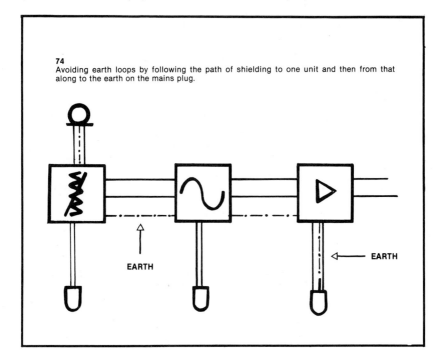

74
Avoiding earth loops by following the path of shielding to one unit and then from that along to the earth on the mains plug.

EARTH

EARTH

Loudspeaker Wiring

Loudspeaker signals are stronger than mic or line levels and therefore less susceptible to interference. Nevertheless they must be treated with respect. Speaker cables have two conductors only, which must be colour coded and twisted. The diameter of the conductor depends upon the load and on the cable length but the Association of British Theatre Technicians publishes this guide:

Table 11

8 ohm, 50m up to 100w	0.75 sq mm
8 ohm, 50m, 100w to 400w	2.50 sq mm
8 ohm, 50m, 400 to 1000w	4.00 sq mm
100v line, up to 100w	0.5 sq mm
100v line, 100w to 1000w	1.0 sq mm

Speaker cable does not need to be run in conduit or trunking but it is a good idea to do so. Some local authorities require that 100v line cable is run in metal conduit. Runs should be clear of mains and mic level cables. Generally each takes a different route from stage to central position.

Connectors

There is some controversy on this matter and therefore conflicting standards can be found. Generally, the profession is agreed on mic connectors but not on speaker connectors.

Firstly, it is considered that only a metal covered connector will withstand the battering that theatres can offer and therefore all mic connectors are of the Cannon variety; there are several equivalent makes now available. On no account should jacks be used except in control areas since they cannot withstand the physical damage likely to occur - nor can they reliably remain plugged in. The Cannon connector is provided with a locking clip so that the cable cannot come unplugged.

Mic level signal carriers are usually male, which carry even numbers on the chart. The actual connector (called an XLR connector), has 3 pins for the shield and two conductors, and an even number to denote the type of plug involved. Thus a plug on a cable would be XLR - 3 - I2c whereas a panel mounted plug would be XLR - 3 - 32. The earth is connected to pin 1, positive conductor to pin 2, and negative conductor to pin 3.

Speaker connectors can be jacks but Cannons are more popular, they are tougher and can carry the high current associated with big loudspeaker systems.

In the past 4 pin Cannons have been recommended since this accommodates both 100v line and low impedance systems on one connector - both requiring two pins each. However, confusion has now become common since some people prefer 3 pin connectors - others link pins so that higher currents can be carried. There is no current standard.

It may therefore be desirable to use terminal blocks for permanently installed loudspeakers. Portable equipment can still use Cannons for durability providing that clear indication is given of how they are wired so that there is no confusion when other equipment is hired.

Connections by XLR and jack to the rear of a theatre mixer.

Mains Supplies

The main feature of mains supplies for sound equipment is that they should separate from all others in the building. This means being separate in such a way that disturbances in other supplies caused by contactors on heating and ventilation systems cannot effect the sound systems. Mains supplies free of such disturbances are knowns as 'clean feed', and should be requested for all sound equipment. All plugs and sockets should be 13A, correctly fused to their load. A liberal number of outlets is desirable, they should have neon indicators and be engraved 'clean feed sound mains' or otherwise similarly identifed. It should not be forgotten that equipment is occasionally positioned in unusual locations and so sockets should be available around the stage, orchestra pit, apron and slips.

It is especially important to ensure maximum protection for musicians using electrical instruments; accidents with electric guitars are frequently fatal. An old method of protection was the provision of an isolating transformer, but this is not effective if several instruments are fed from the same transformer.

Current practice is to provide sensitive current balance circuit breakers for each circuit—communications, sound system, orchestra sockets, auditorium sockets and stage sockets. These devices switch off the power when a fault is detected; often the fault is such that the fuse will not blow and earthing is faulty, a potentially lethal situation. The ABTT publishes an excellent leaflet on this subject and advises that each breaker should operate at not more than 30 milliamp and not more than 30 milliseconds.

A common problem is the matching of mains connectors and the ABTT also advises the provision of outlet boxes, containing the available connectors, 5A, 13A and 15A, and fed through the circuit breakers. This obviates changing plugs which is time consuming and occasionally dangerous where pressure of work can cause carelessness.

It is particularly important to check fuses and connections of all incoming equipment. Touring groups are notoriously lax about safety, and fame is no guarantee of good maintenance. Under the terms of the Health and Safety Act, there are no exclusion causes for theatre managers and their staff.

Budgets, Tenders and Specifications

Finally, of course, it comes down to money, the most important aspect of any specification. Yet it is strange how few people remember to—or are content to—let it be known how much they have to spend. The result is usually that quotations are presented with vastly differing costs and, in the absence of qualified advice, most councils or managers will opt for the lowest; perhaps they are obliged to do so anyway. But it is often not the wisest move.

We have to start with the specification. Few people really understand a technical data sheet in detail and therefore are unable to judge one manufacturer's equipment from the next,—except on price which reflects overheads and prestige value in addition to component cost and expertise.

Sound equipment varies widely in price, but it rarely varies in quality within a price level. In other words it is one of the few fields where you can be sure of obtaining value for money. A loudspeaker at £400 really does sound better than one at £100. But a council cannot make a judgement on price alone—especially with the lowest acceptance clause around.

The first step is that managers and boards have to know more about sound equipment—perhaps just enough to appreciate the differences in equipment: no-one is suggesting that they should design their own systems. In many respects an outside consultant is the answer to this. Only he may marry the theatre's needs to a system design without pressure from commercial interests. Only he can judge independently which parts of which quotations match the specification. Consider that a system may be installed for many years; comprises a large capital expense; and is a vital part of the presentation of the product. To leave such matters in the hands of manufacturers alone is foolish. Few manufacturers in England relate their designs to the specific acoustic of the auditorium in question. Most produce a system patchy in quality—a good mixer say but less satisfactory loudspeakers. Remember the weak link theory.

The only effective way to produce a good balanced system is to specify the best right through—perhaps different manufacturers for each section—but only a consultant can match the items with true independence. It is true that a good electrician can also do this but his knowledge of equipment available will not be as far-reaching, and he may be too close to the problems to see many answers.

Ideally, the council and manager should lay out a brief: An understanding of what the system is basically required to achieve and specifying quantities of microphones, tape decks etc., required. At this point it is vital to think ahead, few other fields have grown so fast as sound. In 1966 the Palladium was provided with a 20 channel mixer; ten years later they were talking in terms of 50 ways and above. Think ahead as far as possible and include as many extra mics, speakers and control channels as possible; include spare ways in the wiring, extra speaker lines and mic lines. Include the type of productions you haven't yet had—they might come in the life of the next system. Make the next system flexible and expandable. The consultant should then produce a document containing his understanding of the brief which should be checked with the client before the next stage is reached. This is the system design stage itself.

Here the consultant should be free to discuss his ideas with several manufacturers, to ensure that they make known to him not only what is the most up to date equipment available but also how much can be achieved without incurring extra costs for specialised items.

This discussion is a vital part of the system design stage. Many consultants put too much detail into the specification and adhere to it rigidly. The result is that the system usually costs more, without the opportunity of the manufacturer feeling involved in its growth.

Once the consultant has pooled his ideas with the manufacturers, he is ready to draw up the specification—an example appears in the appendix—and it should be checked with the client before it is considered complete. Maybe new problems have arisen meanwhile, second thoughts have occurred or the consultant has emphasised one aspect more than necessary.

Tenders should be submitted in two envelopes, one for specifications which is opened first, the other for prices which is only opened if the first is correct. This is the fairest method to avoid deviations and temptations of lowest prices.

For example, consider that the spec calls for a line source column speaker with frequency response 40-16kHz $\pm$ 3dB and having a sound pressure level of 90dB at 3 ,1watt input. There would be more items in the spec but that is the basis. Should a manufacturer come back with a unit having the same frequency response but quoting 35watts rms instead of a SPL figure, **then he has not matched the spec.** It is possible that the unit produces less than the acceptable SPL, so the manufacturer in question should be asked to quote a SPL figure. Only by complete comparison based on an agreed independent spec can the money be fairly spent.

In choosing the manufacturer there is more to consider—how long have they been in operation; are they financially stable; are they likely to merge or be taken over in the near future; what is the service agreement; is there an out-of-hours back-up system; how far away are they.

At this point, the consultant's job reaches a supervisory phase since many problems can occur on site, however well the system was designed in the first place—and, in any case, there will be rewiring to supervise.

Remembering the weak link theory again indicates that the cabling is a vital part of the system and must be specified. Possibly some existing cabling can be used but that consideration will have to come out of contractor/consultant discussion. The complete requirement should be specified first.

Finally, the consultant should deal with staff training, operation and maintenance and ensure that manufacturers have provided the required spares and handbooks.

All this costs money, of course, and sound system budgets have been notoriously low, as we have said earlier. The figure included in annual estimates is usually a manager's guess—often at one in the morning, before presentation, when qualified advice is denied him. The only real way is to secure advice in good time; most consultants or manufacturers can provide "guesstimate" figures good enough for budget purposes without going into the detail above. If the committee will not wear the figure in one year then spread it over two and have the system installed at the end of one year—into the next. But make sure all understand the way it is being done. Many a phased scheme like this has been vetoed later because someone thought last year's mixer purchase was all there was to it. Discuss different methods of payment with manufacturers. Most offer a credit purchase deal through independent finance houses, others give discount for cash with order. Yet another way is to hire a system for a particular show—allocating much of the cost to that show—and then keep it on long term decreasing hire with an option to purchase after a few months. In this way, before purchase is negotiated, changes in the system can be easily made until the best compromise is reached.

Talk to the Arts Council—it is possible that grants could be available—certainly this has happened in several major touring theatres.

Consider also the maintenance aspect—not only will the system need an annual overhaul but possibly equipment can be purchased as a replacement for the saving of repair costs. This is certainly done with smaller items like microphones which go down as maintenance replacements not capital expenditure. Consider buying spare parts and assembling units yourselves. There are many many legitimate ways to make the best use of limited resources.

The best advice is repeated from Francis Reid's excellent book **The Staging Handbook**—'above all budgets must not only be realistic but agreed by all to be so.' Otherwise what is the point of having them?

Section Five
Some sample problems

Swimming Pools and Churches

Although we are primarily concerned with entertainment sound, which suggests theatre buildings, sufficient activity is taking place in sports and religious buildings to warrant our attention. Essentially, they have one common problem—long reverberation times which obscure all but the slowest speech. This is one reason that church services contain long, slow syllable phrasing.

In these areas, it is a mistake to introduce high sound levels from a small number of locations. The only answer is to provide as many sources as possible and keep the sound level very low. Ideally no one would be far from a loudspeaker. This does, of course, suggest that the directional effect has to be sacrificed although in churches some realism can be maintained by providing delay lines thus:

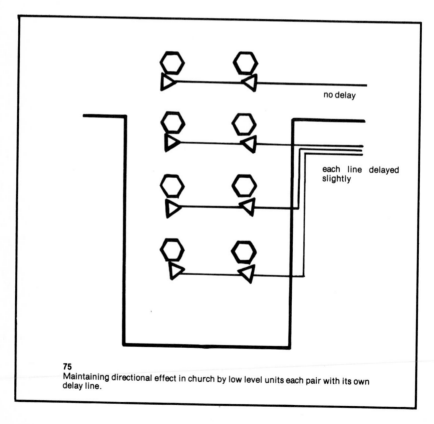

no delay

each line delayed slightly

75
Maintaining directional effect in church by low level units each pair with its own delay line.

In these areas we would usually be dealing with speech only systems and reinforcement level rather than high level. There is some argument for using restricted frequency systems to prevent much low frequency sound from reverberating. The BBC-designed column, mentioned earlier, is a useful guide at 100Hz - 8kHz. A graphic equaliser is especially valuable in such locations since standing waves can create havoc with feedback and corrections are necessary. The voice can also be given some 'attack' in this way since the mixer is likely to be simpler in these cases and lack extensive equalisation.

Directional microphones are essential to prevent the pickup of background noise and cut down feedback, and directional speakers are also required which would normally mean columns. There are several small 'speech only' columns on the market which should not be used in these situations since their reduced size prevents the beam from being very directional—the longer the column the more directional it will be. Some professional church reinforcement systems use speakers 10' long.

Outdoor Systems

We have seen that the shape and treatment of surfaces in a room can create good or bad acoustics; reverberation times which are a help or a hindrance. Generally outdoor events take place well away from structures and therefore there are no reflections and reverberation time is nil. The air is the only tool at the designer's disposal and it is important that the effects of wind and temperature are understood. It is often said that sound carries when the wind is blowing towards the listener. This is an erroneous assumption.

What actually happens when the wind and sound are travelling in the same direction is that wind cools the lower levels of air causing the sound waves to be refracted downwards towards the listener. Wind blowing against the sound causes sound waves to be refracted upwards and away from the listener. Therefore loudspeakers for open air events should always be pointing with the prevailing wind to cover the largest area.

Another important aspect is that of the necessary sound pressure level. We have seen earlier that this must be more than the level of the ambient noise, and outdoor events frequently generate 70dB at least in this category. A loudspeaker producing 110dB at 4' with full power could be heard nearly 300' away before the background level of 70dB became dangerous. This distance would certainly cover many events, but even so it is often wiser to provide more speakers for even coverage at lower levels.

It is especially important that the speakers relate to the movement or otherwise of the listener; they must face the same way or else wind movements and time delays induced by distance can create disturbing echoes.

Where there is some structure, either natural or man-made, it is important to use it as a supportive reflecting surface by focussing the sound away from the surface and not towards it—a process that would create reflections. There is good evidence to suggest some of the greatest outdoor orations were set against natural cliffs; we have also seen how the Greek theatre orchestra was set against a reflective wall.

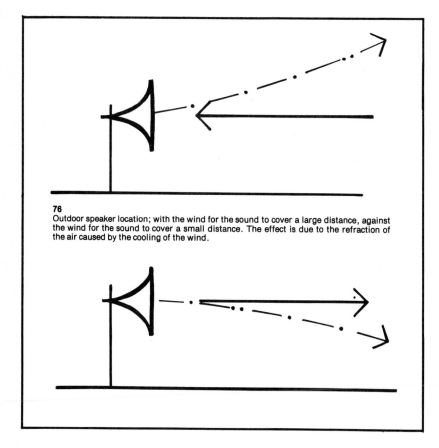

76
Outdoor speaker location; with the wind for the sound to cover a large distance, against the wind for the sound to cover a small distance. The effect is due to the refraction of the air caused by the cooling of the wind.

Where the ground slopes it is vital to use it as the Greeks did and create a natural auditorium, thus:

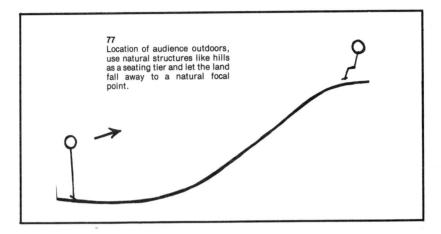

77
Location of audience outdoors, use natural structures like hills as a seating tier and let the land fall away to a natural focal point.

Helping those outdoors to see and hear. A stand at Hidcote Manor.

Equipment outdoors must obviously be weatherproof and this suggests the metal horn speaker in preference to the flimsier moving coil type. Good quality horns are available in speech frequencies and they will come as a surprise to the listeners' usual expectation of thin, tinny public address normally associated with outdoor events. As with most pieces of sound equipment—good units are not cheap. The choice, and use, of microphone is important. It still has to be cardioid even though there is no reverberant acoustic and little chance of feedback. There is, however, much background noise that we do not want picked up. Mics should always have some wind filter fitted, and are frequently used too close to the mouth and with too much level so that distortion results. It is vital that the excitement of the moment is conveyed without shouting. There are some close talk commentator's mics available—also known as lip mics—and these are preferable to ordinary cardioid.

Outdoor events are, by their nature, temporary and great care is needed in rigging and connecting. It is wise to ensure spares are available and not to run one circuit of speakers round the ground from one amplifier. Several circuits from several amps might be more expensive but it is more flexible, more balanced and safer.

Theatre In The Round and Thrust Stages
Firstly, let us establish the shapes that we have in mind with respect to these two terms:

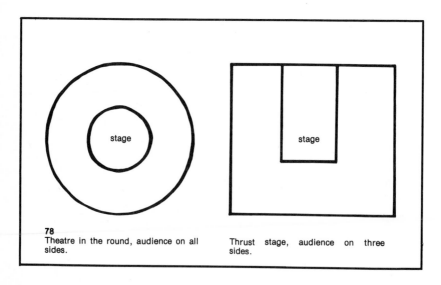

78
Theatre in the round, audience on all sides.

Thrust stage, audience on three sides.

Secondly let us consider the scale of the problem. In small auditoria the intelligibility contour created by the performer will be likely to encompass all the seats, even those behind him, and it can be no accident that some of the most successful theatres of this type have been modest in size.

A small theatre in the round needing no reinforcement of the voice since all seats are within the intelligibility contour.

By comparison, a large auditorium creates problems since some people will be outside the intelligibility contour and will therefore not hear clearly. There is some evidence that large auditoria of this type have occasionally utilised discreet reinforcement, but the subject is usually a sore point and questions are not popular. With performers now located in the auditoria, the two main problems are avoidance of feedback and maintenance of directability. Feedback can be minimised by using the techniques we have already discussed—directional mics and speakers—room equalisation. The directional effect can be maintained by careful speaker location and sensible mixing, again using techniques already discussed.

In these shapes there is no pros wall on which to mount speakers, the backstage wall of the thrust stage being too far back for correct directability and dangerous for feedback. The only possible location therefore is over the stage area itself - radiating outwards. The units should be very directional so that there are no unwanted reflections; there is no sound going back into the mic again. This will inevitably lead to the use of many units. As with a conventional system, the questions of desired SPL over wide or narrow range will determine speaker choice - bins/horns, monitors or columns. Horns are especially useful in these situations.

Mics should be more directional than normal, probably short rifle mics around stage edge with long rifles overhead. The mixer channels should have good mid equalisation on these channels since it will be recalled that rifle mics can lack presence in some situations.

Mixers for this work should be more complex than normal if some authenticity is required as to direction since mics are usually mixed with slight predominance to their local area speaker as well as to the others in some degree. This means that there should be output for each stage area.

In musicals, the main vocal, hand and orchestra mics could be fed stereo, as may the reinforcement mics - but this is rare, generally they are mixed equally to all areas.

Since there are so many outputs, equalisation of room acoustics is expensive, but is the only way of evening out the peaks and troughs and providing more gain before feedback. Musicals require foldback to artists on stage and these are also best overhead, but feedback is likely and sundry measures have to be taken, frequen-

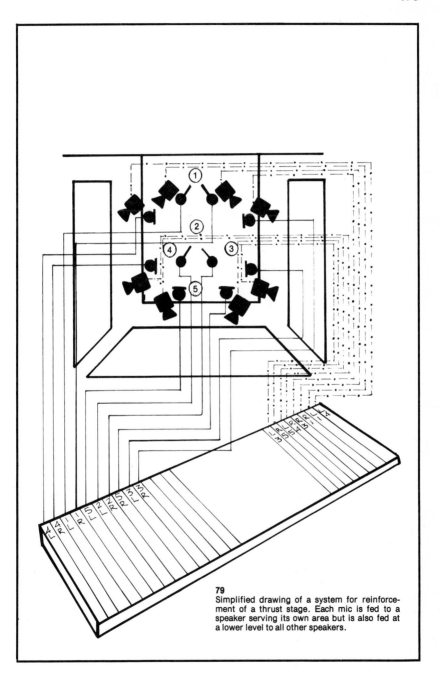

79
Simplified drawing of a system for reinforcement of a thrust stage. Each mic is fed to a speaker serving its own area but is also fed at a lower level to all other speakers.

cy shifters often giving just the extra bit of level required.

These design principles work just as well in large arena systems although another approach would be to cut down the power of the centre speaker array in favour of a second circle of units working to time delay. This is especially the case if the arena is very reverberant. It should be appreciated that the delay is provided to prevent several sound paths from overlapping and 'muddying' the sound, rather than to preserve the directional effect which in large venues sometimes has to take second place to clarity.

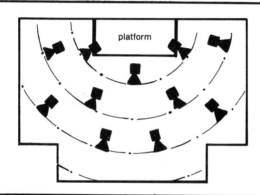

80 IN A LARGE ARENA
in a large arena it might be preferable to install overhead speakers related to the radius of time delay, 40' further out each time. The aim is not so much to maintain a directional effect as to prevent muddying of the sound by allowing several sound paths to arrive at the listener at different times. The fourth ring would not have speakers for the sake of economy but would be adequately served by the third ring speakers.

A concert taking place in a sports hall. A network of suspended units with delay or of portable floor speakers is the only way to overcome these difficult acoustics.

One of the main problems with these areas is that speakers need to be in view, and this upsets architects. It is important to explain why this position is unavoidable and to work together on some shape and colour that is the least objectionable. It is especially important to overcome the view that good sound is impossible in large venues so speaker positions do not matter. Indeed in the realms of large venue/poor acoustics, good positions are as vital as ever.

Today, large venues are the only location for expensive stars who need vast audiences to support high expenses. Conversely, big stars may appear live so seldom that vast audiences are likely. Concerts can take place in areas previously unconsidered as locations for music, with consequent acoustic problems. In these cases it is vital that the planners all get together—and that includes those responsible for the seating layout, since the acoustician may deem it necessary to drape walls or voids to cut down reverberation, and speakers may need some overhead support relative to seating tiers.

Production schedules must be planned to accommodate long fit ups and balancing of sound systems.

In general terms, high-quality high-level sound systems are too expensive for any large venue to consider their purchase. The problem is the requirement of both large quantities of speakers and amplifiers, and of expensive and complex delay and equalisation backup. Systems toured by popular stars for such areas frequently cost well over £100,000.

An array of speakers including bass bins, mid range and HF horns typical to the rock industry.

Touring

Since the provision of good equipment by theatres is patchy, for a variety of reasons based on economics, it is often preferable for companies to tour their own system. This also overcomes compatibility problems with alien plugs and sockets and ensures some consistency in sound effects and mixing since the same operator is working with the same system throughout the life of the show.

The obvious requirement of equipment going on tour is that it should be robust and capable of withstanding the most violent handling. Crews are often not respectful of equipment being removed from a theatre in pouring rain at two o'clock in the morning. The most sensible provision is that of the 'flight'case—an aluminium box lined with foam rubber cut to the shape of the equipment it holds. Wheels and handles on such boxes not only make life easier for the crew but can prevent mishandling.

Plugs and cables come in for the most misuse, and spare parts, including spare made up cables, are essential as well as a well-equipped tool kit. Equipment is now available to test cables and connectors in order to locate faults quickly, but patience on the get-out when uncoiling and unplugging is the best protection.

On no account should any venue come as a surprise, a prior visit is vital to check mains supplies, connectors and locations; house sound system (as back up); house electrical staff; local service source; acoustics. It is especially useful to seek the opinions of local staff on dead spots and other acoustics problems. Five minutes chat can save hours wasted experimenting.

Above all it is vital that there is time to set up the system properly and tune it to the house acoustic. If there is not time to do this there is little point in touring a system, since the result would be unlikely to justify the effort and expense involved.

One thorny problem is that of the location of the sound mixing desk. We have seen that it is desirable for this to be located in the auditorium, but in some venues this can come as a shock to managements, especially when accompanied with untidy cabling. Prior discussion on this is vital, both to prevent the sale of relevant seats and work out cable runs that won't upset the manager or the local safety officer. We have also seen that all systems require to be fed by current-balance earth-leakage circuit-breakers. Electrical installations, maintenance and regulations vary widely and these devices are essential for ensuring safety.

It is an especially good idea to keep an index of venues used with both data and comments in preparation for the next visit. On no account should such details be confined to one person's memory.

Low Ceilings

If we consider the normal approach to sound system design applied to a room with a low ceiling, we find that the speaker beam cannot reach to the rear without absorption by those seated nearby.

We have mentioned earlier that a small column speaker, which might be considered a solution to this problem, would not act as a full column in radiating sound, nor would it be likely to have a good frequency response for multipurpose use. The only answer therefore is to mount a number of single drivers in the ceiling itself. An 8″ diameter unit provides quite an acceptable sound in a very small ceiling cavity although it would be desirable to provide higher quality cabinets in good full range installations. Where there is no ceiling cavity, it is worth considering surface mounting small cabinet units for improved dispersion rather than the more immediate solution of small wall-mounted columns.

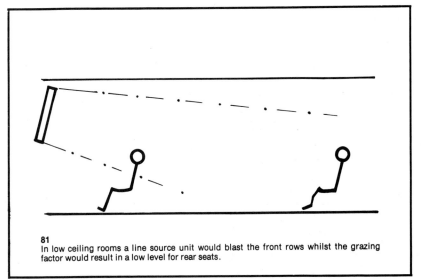

81
In low ceiling rooms a line source unit would blast the front rows whilst the grazing factor would result in a low level for rear seats.

In all cases it is vital to achieve a good, even coverage of sound—the directional effect being momentarily ignored. To this end the speaker beams should intersect at ear level.

In a large, low ceiling area, the difference in multiple sound paths might be such that time delay systems are needed. Remember that a difference of more than 40' in sound paths produces a distinct echo so a delay on amplified sound is needed.

In some cases these rooms cannot have one fixed focal point. This creates two problems. First the likelihood of a mic being positioned under a speaker and thus generating howl-round. Second the delay network above is worthless unless altered each time.

The first problem is easier to solve by simply switching off the speaker closest to the mic. The second is more complex although solvable if the different locations of focus, hence the relationship of sound paths, are predictable and repeated. Once the delay setting and gain setting is known for each format it can be set up each time.

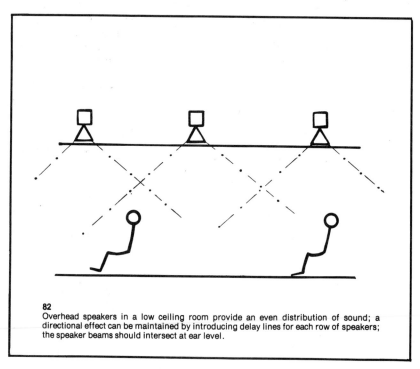

82
Overhead speakers in a low ceiling room provide an even distribution of sound; a directional effect can be maintained by introducing delay lines for each row of speakers; the speaker beams should intersect at ear level.

Banquets

Banquets usually take place either in what we may have described above—a low ceiling room—a restaurant, exhibition gallery, studio, theatre or foyer.

In these events the location of the top table—presumed location of the speechmaker—is paramount. It is especially useful if this can be located on a raised platform—perhaps on stage if it is not required for dance band or cabaret. A good sightline will help acoustics and the reception of the speech.

If there is a system installed in the room it is generally facing the wrong way and likely to feedback when the mic is turned up. This may appear a detail but many a speech has been hampered by the sound creeping up behind the audience. In general it is best to avoid the house system and provide portable speakers on good stands in the body of the hall itself. These can thus be positioned to help the directional effect, reduce feedback, and angled to avoid reflections and standing waves.

Since most speechmakers need to address people over a wide angle it is desirable to provide two microphones to cover all the arc of speech. In this case the polarity—the way in which each mic is wired—needs careful checking, since opposing wiring will cause signal cancellations.

Banquets are frequently accompanied by cabaret or disco and it is wiser to accept each function must have its own system. This may mean untidy cables, but does not put all the eggs in one basket, and ensures all relevant criteria are met. A speech system is not a disco system is not a cabaret system.

Summary

There is a tendency for the sound system in ad hoc performance areas to be of a lower standard than those in more traditional surroundings. There is really no valid reason for this, if the basic principles of acoustics and system design are observed. Consider the reverberation of the area and whether a low level system would be more desirable. Consider how important is the preservation of the directional effect. Perhaps it should be sacrificed for the sake of clarity and ease of speaker positioning. Do not forget that one portable speaker correctly placed can be worth several hidden away but in the wrong positions.

Section Six

Effects

The sound that we have been concerned with so far is that produced from a live source, whether in the sound reinforcement of speech or in the more sophisticated form of vocal and instrument amplification on musicals and concerts. Now we will turn our attention to systems reproducing recorded sound.

First let us examine the function of such systems. They may be for the reproduction of speech, music, sound effects or film. In each case the first step is to examine the desired frequency response of the source. Speech will have the narrowest frequency band, then film, and music cum effects. Such analysis will affect the choice of speakers through which the recording is played.

In simple terms all four sources may be played through any wide range system, whether bass bin/horn or monitor; but only speech is likely to remain unaffected if played through most column speakers, whose narrower frequency response would alter music and sound effects. Film sound under such conditions could be acceptable but it would be unlikely to be of high quality. A good quality foldback speaker can sometimes be used for effects. Generally it is desirable to. provide a separate system for recorded sound, working alongside that provided for live sound. The sources can be mixed and controlled by the same mixer that deals with microphone channels but they would require separate outputs. These would feed either the main wide range system or a separate effects system of wide range units, most of which should be portable so that they may be best related to the scenery and apparent direction of the sound effect they produce.

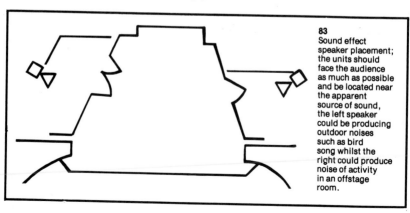

83
Sound effect speaker placement; the units should face the audience as much as possible and be located near the apparent source of sound, the left speaker could be producing outdoor noises such as bird song whilst the right could produce noise of activity in an offstage room.

We have spoken earlier about stereo and quadrophonic sound, it is here that these terms really become involved.

In the case of music reproduction it is unlikely that the recording would be made from a live orchestra since a quality recording would be difficult to obtain except in fully professional circumstances. The source is more likely to be either a taping of one or two instruments, in which case mono is the most usual, or taken from a disc in which case it will already be stereo. Thus we have either a single track, mono, or music which could easily be fed into the sound system so that it radiates equally from both sides of the pros arch, or a conventional stereo set-up, with the disadvantage mentioned earlier that only those at the apex of the speaker triangle will be receiving true stereo. It is possible that this effect may not be as damaging in recorded music as it could be in the amplification of live sound.

A quadrophonic system would add the rear two corners, or at least two extra channels, to the stereo picture. This particular situation would be suitable where it was felt desirable to involve the audience more than usual and where there is much scope for sound effects. The usual example is the play "Journey's End" where the sounds of battle assail the audience on all sides.

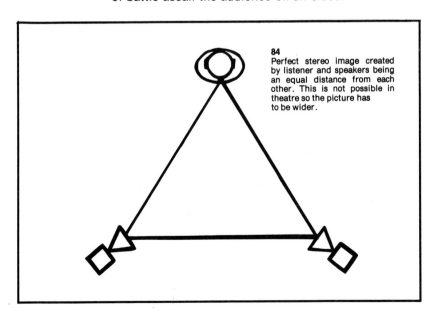

84
Perfect stereo image created by listener and speakers being an equal distance from each other. This is not possible in theatre so the picture has to be wider.

This illustrates the main danger of sound effects—that of producing something so realistic, unusual or startling that the audience is distracted from the play into wondering about the source or method of the effect itself. At all times the effects should blend with other aspects of the production.

As mentioned earlier, a simpler way of achieving almost the same result is to produce a mono sound source and fade it around from one speaker to the next. This is easier to record than stereo or quad effects and especially suited to moving objects like cars or planes.

Some people may recall that original sound effects were recorded on 78 rpm discs which were played on twin turntables known as a panatrope. Although heavy and fragile the main advantage of this system was that all effects were equally accessible. Today the effects are recorded on magnetic tape, a method that is more precise but lacks random access, so that the tape has frequently to be edited during rehearsal.

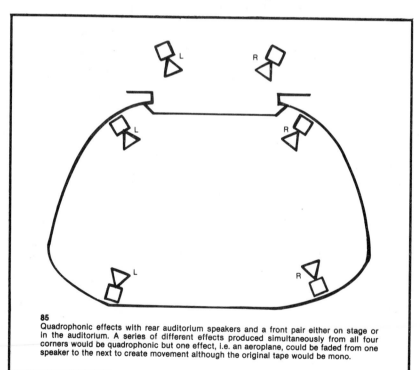

85
Quadrophonic effects with rear auditorium speakers and a front pair either on stage or in the auditorium. A series of different effects produced simultaneously from all four corners would be quadrophonic but one effect, i.e. an aeroplane, could be faded from one speaker to the next to create movement although the original tape would be mono.

Each piece of tape containing an effect is separated from another by means of a leader tape. This should be coloured differently to the recording tape and care should be taken not to overlook the dim and coloured lighting of operating positions. The nature of the effect should be written on the leader with chinagraph pencil. Most professional tape decks are fitted with a method of automatically stopping the movement of the tape once the effect has been played. Recent units are fitted with a light sensitive cell and a small bulb, the light being allowed to pass from one to the other by the insertion in the effects tape of clear tape. Older machines were fitted with a split ring containing part of the stop circuit, which was completed when a metal foil tape was inserted into the effects tape. Although these devices are a considerable help, they are by no means totally reliable and the sound operator should be always on his guard.

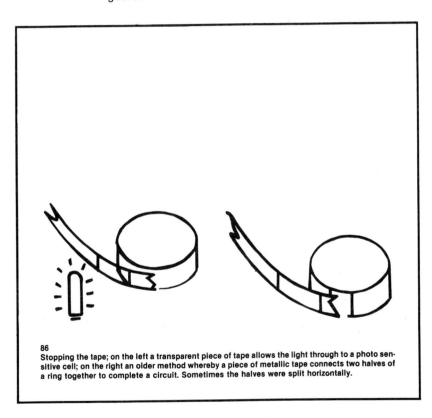

86
Stopping the tape; on the left a transparent piece of tape allows the light through to a photo sensitive cell; on the right an older method whereby a piece of metallic tape connects two halves of a ring together to complete a circuit. Sometimes the halves were split horizontally.

Like the rest of the system, the choice of tape deck is another area where the purchaser obtains accurate value for money. The expensive professional models offer genuine improvements over their cheaper counterparts. Unlike domestic models, professional recorders have three heads, erase, record and play. This means that a recording can easily be monitored as it is made; it also means that some degree of echo is possible by feeding the monitored playback to the recording head again.

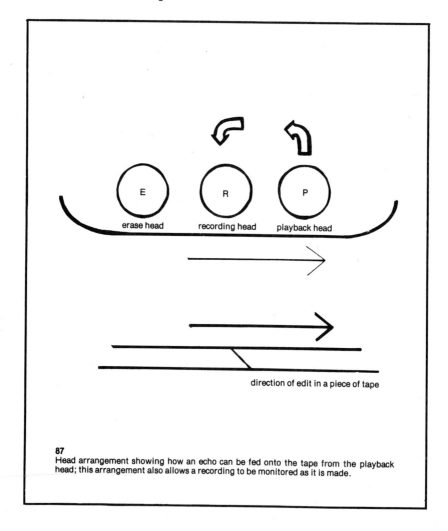

87
Head arrangement showing how an echo can be fed onto the tape from the playback head; this arrangement also allows a recording to be monitored as it is made.

A professional tape recorder will allow plenty of access to the heads so that the tape may be easily edited as it passes the playback head. The tape should be moved back and forward by hand so that the precise position of sound and silence can be judged. Cuts are made with special non-metallic scissors, or razor blades, and always at an angle to overcome noise on a join - this also prevents splices from coming undone. Special jointing tape and blocks are used.

A popular professional tape machine; access to the heads for easy editing is vital.

A copy should always be made of the completed, edited tape. Often sound effects are continuous—birdsong being a typical example. In these cases a loop of tape is made, taking care not to produce a 'click' join or distinctive effect which would easily give the game away as it was repeated. Some designers are happy to use loops in the show—taking care that they cannot snag on the machine or adjacent items. Others prefer to use the loop to record whatever length of effect is required and cut this into the main tape. Loops are moved solely by the capstan and not by the reel motors, therefore some professional machines have the facility to switch these off.

The process of recording makes use of the fluctuating magnetic field created by the fluctuating current at the recording head. This 'assembles' the tiny 'magnets' on the tape into a pattern which is readable by the playback head. The more tiny 'magnets' that pass the recording head in any second, the better will be the frequency response of the recording, so the faster the better. Speech is acceptable at 3¾ ips but preferable at 7½ ips which is the speed at which most theatre effects and music are recorded. Improvements in performance are happening constantly. Some professional machines are two speed, others three, the full speed range being 1⅞, 3¾, 7½, 15 ips. Some machines can be fitted with a speed variation control which greatly facilitates the creation of effects.

Since control positions are frequently full of equipment, it is unlikely that the tape machine will be immmediately accessible, therefore remote control over the basic functions is often provided. Again, like the auto stop, this facility is not 100% reliable but acceptable, the machine should however be visible and reasonably accessible. Since machines frequently work within the audience's hearing, their operation also needs to be silent.

It is wise to think in terms of two machines. Sometimes effects overlap, such as those of continuous birdsong with spot effects. On other occasions it is a good idea to play background music as the audience enter—especially in light entertainment. This really needs to be capable to playing well after the normal curtain up time, in case of a late start—hence the first effect should be lined up ready on the other machine.

So far we have spoken of reel-to-reel machines and not of cartridge or cassette machines, whose domestic versions are more familiar to the general public. Although these devices are improving constantly they do not offer the flexibility in editing of reel-to-reel units. It is conceivable, however, that background music and some effects might not require ultra high standards of frequency response. Hence music could certainly be played-from cassette although professionally-made recording is more likely to have a lower noise level than one made 'in house'. Cartridges too have their uses in the spot effect field - their prime function in pop radio broadcasting. So the hold of the traditional reel-to-reel machine is slowly being broken.

Disc units are seldom used for shows but useful for making up tapes. Again good quality is important: transcription standard with stroboscopic speed check and at least two speed—33 rpm and 45. 78 rpm is very rare but some shows do demand the use of old records. Theatres who receive productions from local amateurs frequently find music and effects tapes made on machines alien to that particular theatre. Here it is a good idea to have a special input panel of all the sockets available. Cannon, Din, jack, phono etc., so that their machines may feed into the system. A gain control on the input would be required to ensure that the signal produced does not overload the next stage—i.e. the mixer or amplifier.

The use of sound effects is governed by the same law as that affecting lighting effects—don't get too enthusiastic. The effects should help the performance not distract from it. Some spectacular distractions occur from the production of live effects. Before the advent of recording, all effects were live but today few remain. Two areas that require such an approach being bells and weather.

In the first case few sound systems can accurately reproduce the attack and the harmonics of a bell. Location of such a directional sound is also often a problem with speakers being difficult to hide on the set. Hence clock chimes, doorbells, telephones and even church bells are often produced live, recordings being used only in complex or unusual cases. Timing is vital here since telephones should not ring after being answered and ideally should be wired so they cannot. Small speakers can be concealed in the handset for real authenticity. The effects of weather can be produced by recording but they are seldom convincing. One problem is that a recording implies a degree of repetition which is not present in reality. Rain can be represented by the movement of dried peas in a box, wind by the turning of

a slatted drum against canvas and thunder by the rattle
of a piece of suspended sheet steel.

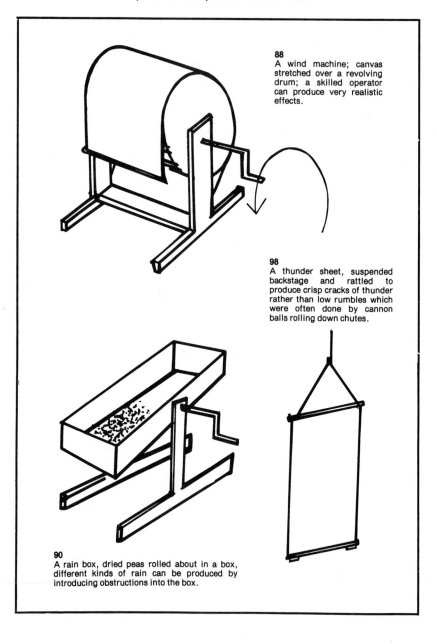

88
A wind machine; canvas
stretched over a revolving
drum; a skilled operator
can produce very realistic
effects.

98
A thunder sheet, suspended
backstage and rattled to
produce crisp cracks of thunder
rather than low rumbles which
were often done by cannon
balls rolling down chutes.

90
A rain box, dried peas rolled about in a box,
different kinds of rain can be produced by
introducing obstructions into the box.

Other 'noises off' include the door slam—literally a small door offstage mounted on a base board—and the effect of feet treading non-wooden surfaces such as gravel—simply created by treading in a small tray filled with the stones.

Live effects are sometimes amplified but care should be taken with the frequency response of the system otherwise much of the quality will be lost as mentioned at the start of this section.

The amplification of live effects, does not inhibit their spontaneity.

Communications
If sound system budgets are the poor relation of theatre financing, then communication budgets are a long-forgotten relation. There can be few other ways of false economy.

Theatre management is about balancing budgets, and bad communication can waste the most important commodity the theatre has at its disposal—time.

Production Communications
Just as there are two phases in a production—rehearsal and performance—so are there two different types of contact required.

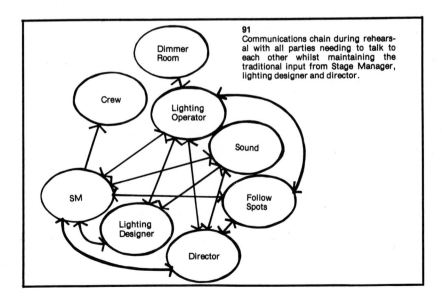

91
Communications chain during rehearsal with all parties needing to talk to each other whilst maintaining the traditional input from Stage Manager, lighting designer and director.

Firstly we have to appreciate the directions in which information needs to flow at rehearsal time. The stage manager needs to talk to all his crew, and they to him, to query instructions and raise problems. The lighting designer needs to talk to the lighting operator and follow-spot positions and they need to be able to go back to him. The lighting operator needs to talk to the dimmer room, and vice-versa, for maintenance during working—changing fuses, repairing dimmers etc. The director too may require some communication—certainly with the stage manager, but on complex productions he may prefer to talk straight to the crew and bypass the stage manager. Finally there may be a need for sound operators and designers to talk from equipment positioned backstage to the control desk and to monitoring positions on other tiers.

So we have four chains of communication simultaneously with a requirement for the s.m. (stage manager) to override into all chains. Consider that most crew will require their hands free to operate some equipment—this means that the method of contact should be available without touch—and similarly their reply.

Ring Intercoms

The answer is the headset which is fitted with a small boom mic. The unit is fed from a small amplifier either belt mounted or built into a wall unit and containing volume controls and frequently a variety of ways of in-

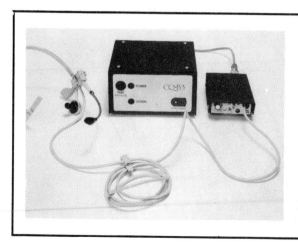

Intercom system for ring communication showing belt pack on right and lightweight headset and mic on left.

dicating that the unit is being contacted—via an indicator light, or ways of indicating to others that they are being contacted.

Each position would then have one of these units and the usual system is that all mics and headsets are live so that a complete conversation may be carried out by all wearers. This is vital at rehearsal times when queries result. Usually only the s.m. will be talking but others need the facility to do so too.

Some systems provide 'crashcall' buttons, so that only one mic per chain, say, s.m., lighting designer or director, may talk to that chain and cut out other mics from interrupting. Systems also provide for headsets to receive a selection of chains or a blend. This would be useful in lighting control and follow spots where instructions would emanate normally from the s.m. during rehearsal and show, but alterations may also come from the lighting designer.

This system—known as the ring intercom—has been in use in this country over a number of years but usually only by home made versions using GPO equipment. Now several companies are producing specially made systems and the cost is negligible compared to the benefits. Most small theatres should be accommodated at around £1,300, whilst double would be a reasonable basis for a complex system.

The system is also useful whilst the electrical staff are rigging and focusing lamps. The simple cabling required means that sockets may be inserted anywhere in the line, and lighting galleries, slots and boxes are easily wired for access. The crew member doing the focusing takes the headset around with him and just plugs into the appropriate socket. Voices are saved, tempers kept and time respected.

During performance the number of chains is reduced since only the s.m. is issuing instructions so the system now looks like the diagram following.

Essentially here the talk is outward from the s.m. and crew need only to talk to acknowledge or raise an emergency. This emphasis on single direction communication introduces the other kind often found.

Paging
Paging systems—identified in the past by a well-known brand of speaker on the wall—are far more complex than a simple speaker suggests—perhaps this is why

196

budgets are so low. The cost in complex paging systems is not in the speakers but in the other end—the control.

Of course there are few production areas that may be paged during a performance—perhaps only electric areas—projection room, lighting control and sound room (although the latter really should be open to the theatre acoustic). In these circumstances the s.m. might issue his instructions through the paging speaker—the disadvantage of course being that the other end can't answer back unless other equipment is used.

Paging also would go to dressing rooms either as a whole unit or in groups if stars are involved. There the speaker would also receive a relay of the show from a microphone or microphones suspended downstage. The s.m.'s action of paging brings in a relay which allows his mic to talk and cuts out the show relay. The system reverses when he has finished. Generally the dressing room speaker has a volume control which is fitted only to the show relay chain—not to the s.m. chain. A frequent problem is caused by units having overall volume control so that turning down the show also turns

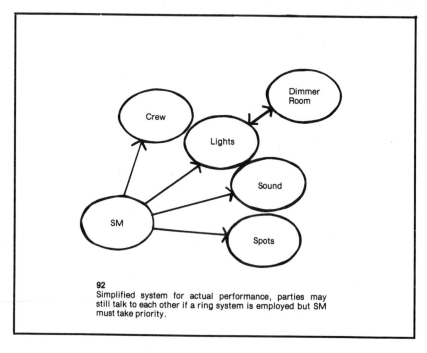

92
Simplified system for actual performance, parties may still talk to each other if a ring system is employed but SM must take priority.

down the s.m. Some units have a preset control that may also be adjusted with a screwdriver. The disadvantage of the s.m. only volume control system is that it requires three wires (and some manufacturers need four) whereas the other less sophisticated systems get by with two.

The s.m. should also be able to page backstage technical areas like crewroom, workshop and scene dock and on large or noisy stages it is an advantage if he can also page the stage itself. In these areas where high sound levels and rough conditions prevail, the horn loudspeaker is best for its rugged appearance and high efficiency. It is also useful if the s.m. can talk to the audience either through the house system or through another simpler system which is preferable since the first method occupies a valuable sound control channel.

Finally the s.m. needs to page the foyer and bars and here great care needs to be taken—more speakers are usually required than is often thought. These areas suffer from very high sound levels and a good balance is required from well-distributed units—not an ineffectual muttering from one discreet box.

In all cases where announcements are repeated, it is worth considering using a cassette recording made under good conditions rather than a hasty muffled announcement made under stress. Female voices are better for this than male because they are clearer and more penetrating.

There is often a requirement for paging to be carried out from another location—say from stage door or front office. This is possible at little extra cost but the system has to be designed so that the s.m. always has priority. Other paging positions are usually supplied with 'engaged' lights when the s.m. speaks.

Cue Lights

A very simple method of indication is light, and the theatre has used this extensively in the past before the growth of sound. Before we look at the system we need to appreciate how the s.m. issues his instructions.

Firstly the production is divided into cues—points where the staff have to carry out some task. Next the s.m. will mark on his prompt copy not only the cue itself, the 'GO', but also a warning several pages or moments in advance 'STAND BY'. During operation the stand by is signalled by a red light and the go by a green light. Both lights on the s.m. desk and on the other end—the outstation—are wired in series so that if one fails, so does the other and the s.m. knows his instruction has not got through.

Cue lights are still useful in areas where verbal communication is not possible, i.e. on stage. Here a portable outstation on long lead may be preferable to a wall box, so that it can be better placed with respect to the set.

The switches on the s.m. desk should have a positive action in keeping with their function and there are ABTT recommendations for colouring and layout.

In recent times various methods of acknowledgement have been applied to the standby circuit since the s.m. frequently needs to know if the outstation is manned and his cue understood. Usually the outstation presses a small button which interrupts the circuit and causes the red light to go out momentarily. Other systems automatically flash until the push is depressed whence they steady.

Detail of a typical stage manager's control panel, cue lights centre, special effects on right, verbal cueing and talkback/paging on top and left.

Radio Systems

Occasionally it is necessary to have communication with a crew member who cannot be connected by cable. Often the crew member is operating scenery on stage, as in the famous trucks in "Blitz" which each contained a stage manager who drove them. In this case, instructions were passed from another stage manager via radio microphone transmitter to receivers in the trucks and on to the operators via an earpiece.

This was an unusual use of this equipment in its day but more people are familiar with radio microphones now and the units are easily linked for such a special occasion. It is possible to complete the chain by fitting the operator with a boom mic and transmitter so that he may talk out to the main stage manager.

Radio microphones are licensed by the Post Office and it is not practical for good quality to use several different channels at the same time. It is possible for communication purposes to tune several receivers to the same transmitter—so several crew members could all hear the same set of instructions.

Telephones

In all the above systems the s.m. features as the fulcrum of the communication. Often, however, one part of the theatre needs to be in touch with another and the telephone is the ideal method. Generally there may be considered three systems: Public, internal, and stage areas. It is desirable to keep the stage areas separate from the others and likely locations are:-

Stage Manager
Front of House
Stage Door
Lighting Control
Sound Control
Flies
Production Desk
Stage Opposite Side
Orchestra Pit
Prop Room

These, of course, are merely suggestions but if the numbers are restricted then these can be easily accommodated on many of the handset units now available. There are two points to make—first those coupled with the ring intercom provide an ideal balance over the old intercom talkback since together they are both versatile and discreet. Second, the stage units require light call as an alternative to bell call for use during performances.

Some telephone systems connect to s.m. desk pushes and are linked to other facilities so that selection of a 'Performance' push cuts out all work lights, selects exits and indicator lights and switches all bells to light call.

The rest of the theatre can be accommodated as a separate system or within a public network—it is a good idea to have coinbox 'phones only in unsupervised parts of the stage area, except for one or two public lines available to recognised priorities like designers and stage managers.

So we have discussed paging, cue lights, ring intercoms and telephones. It is important to understand that for all but the smallest theatre, these are not alternatives but merely different ways of achieving the same end—relevant to the need. Ideally a theatre should be provided with all these systems, not only so that the most appropriate system may be selected for a specific purpose but also in order to provide backup communication in the case of failure.

General Facilities Panels

It is likely therefore that several locations will have many facilities available to them. One consideration in planning the systems has to be access and appearance and in recent years the untidy multitude of small boxes, each carrying a different service, has been replaced by a single box carrying all, served by a single trunking. Consider the lighting control room for example. This will require a show relay speaker with volume control operable only on the relay chain but which also receives the s.m., a socket and volume control for the main ring intercom of the s.m. and another volume control to mix in the lighting designer, a red cue light with acknowledge push and a green cue light, and finally a telephone.

Most stage general facilities panels go further than that and also carry the main sound microphone and loudspeaker sockets as well. Also cue lights and mains outlets for sound equipment.

Under these circumstances it is vital that each system uses a different connector so that no short circuits can be set up.

The Future

Electronics are developing so quickly, and so cheaply, that many people cannot keep pace with the facilities being offered to them, in every increasing numbers and from all sides. The microprocessor enables a variety of functions to be carried out with complete reliability and considerable speed, and the control and processing units are small enough to be accommodated inside most equipment.

In sound terms, the ability of the computer to undertake sophisticated calculations has uncovered defects in early equations used to work out reverberation time. On other fronts the computer can design more efficient speaker systems, generally more compact as well.

The ability to assimilate data at high speed has been well used in sound analysis equipment. Engineers setting up graphic equalisers to even out the house curve—the room acoustics—no longer are dependent on trial and error. Today the analyser provides a display of the strengths of each frequency band, and does so in 'real time' so that the display changes as the equaliser is adjusted.

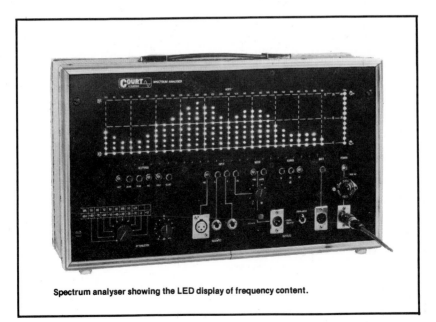

Spectrum analyser showing the LED display of frequency content.

In the recording studio the engineer responsible for mixing the multitrack recording down to the stereo base issued, is assisted by an automated mixer which remembers which tracks were added at various points, and at what amounts.

As with most electronic developments the spin offs eventually affect everyone. Initially sophistication seems beyond most systems but later the facilities become more available as they become cheaper, electronic calculators being a typical example. The use of computers will certainly benefit the design of individual pieces of equipment but it is in the field of control where the most dramatic changes are likely.

It requires little imagination for example to conceive a graphic equaliser coupled with a computer-assisted analyser which would result in automatic room equalisation to a pre-determined pattern. The unit could effect real time changes as the atmosphere, audience and pro-

A section of a computer-assisted mixer.

gramme changed. The result would be a clearer sound, free of feedback except at the highest peaks and even those could be minimised if the unit was programmed accordingly.

The mixer also could benefit from this approach. Here there are basically 3 types of control required—one over programme quality and others over programme volume and routing.

In the first case the 'quality controls'—sensitivity, bass, mid and treble—are seldom adjusted within the space of a musical number or speech. The reason is not the undersirability of doing so. but the problem the operator faces. He is presented with probably over one hundred controls and generally alters them seldom. This is ludicrous where the sound system is supposed to recreate a recording which has perhaps popularised the artist involved, and which originally comprised many tracks of tape taken over several 'takes' of the number and edited or mixed together.

If we return to the recording studio and take a second glance at the automated mixer we may see several basic principles which could shcw the way for theatre mixing consoles.

A set of sensitivity, bass, mid and treble controls linked to a memory system would have the facility of being set to any number of positions and recalled at will by selection of the appropriate memory number. The new settings would then be faded in and the previous ones faded out. The individual controls would still be accessible for immediate adjustments which would not affect the recorded setting unless rerecorded. This is an identical method of operation to that of a stage lighting control. Memories could relate to musical numbers or parts of musical numbers and would be set by the sound consultant during rehearsal.

We have seen earlier that the sound signal takes many routes from the mixer. In addition to the main outputs for vocals—a stereo pair—there will be others perhaps for instruments—again a stereo pair—and yet others for sound effects. Finally there will be at least one foldback chain, probably two or three on larger systems. The process of memorising routing is straightforward and already exists on some systems although it is generally, but not exclusively, limited to straight routing without any degree of level control. The same approach to that of quality control memorising applies here. The benefits would be a tremendous boost for all concerned. An opportunity is here provided for more sophisticated sound effects—several sounds moving simultaneously round the audience. Musicians too are thus offered what they have always demanded—a separate combination of folkback mixes for each musical number or part of the number—previously limited by the dexterity or otherwise of the operator. Again, individual controls would still be provided for immediate adjustment which would not affect the recorded setting unless re-recorded.

The question of controlling programme volume is more complex because the potential for changes is greater than in the areas of quality or routing. Immediate access to the control of each channel is vital. However it should be considered that it is posible to memorise an average level for each channel - again related to a musical number or part number, fading the new levels in and the old levels out. The question of access is solvable by borrowing hardware from lighting controls - the digital wheel. This device protrudes edge-on through the fascia of lighting control desks. Channels recalled from memory onto the wheel are set at their recorded levels, increases in intensity are effected by pushing the wheel forward, reductions by pulling the wheel back. As before the recorded level remains unchanged unless the alteration is re-recorded. It is suggested that if a number of wheels are provided in relationship to the channels involved, momentary alterations can easily be effected as they could on a standard sound desk.

We are now familiar with music recorded in digital fashion where the micro processor is an essential part of the recording studio. There are enormous benefits from this technique in the fidelity of the sound, the lessening of the noise level and in the coordination of the different signals. It may be that the future will see live sound mixing and amplification take place with a totally different base process than that which we are familiar with today. Such a system would require us to adopt a new approach to operating it but it would free us from negotiating feedback and overload, the system would do that itself. It would release us to improve the quality and relevance of the actual sound the audience hears.

Postscript

The chain is now complete.

Every link is vital in achieving a high standard of intelligibility and fidelity. The sound equipment cannot be imposed upon a building, it must be married to the acoustics. The shape and furnishing of the auditorium must be examined and adjusted to assist in the creation of the desired sound. The equipment must be compatible and flexible. The installation must be robust and isolated from other systems likely to cause interference. The operator must be chosen with care—few other technicians have such responsibility. He must be located where he can hear the same sound that the audience hears.

Some of the goals are harder to achieve than others and the temptation to compromise is strong. It must be avoided. A sound system is frequently installed for a life of ten years and it is the most important vehicle for the production's communication with its audience.

The decisions that have to be taken should not be taken in haste or alone. The choice and location of a sound system is a serious and complex matter. Wherever possible professional advice should be sought from those independent of commercial interest. The key improvements to theatre sound over the last ten years are the direct result of the work of a handful of designers and consultants either working alone or in conjunction with sound hire companies. Such interested parties can often suggest and achieve the desired measures to better effect than if the same suggestions were to come from an interested party within the theatre itself.

The purpose of this book is to equip the manager for such debate. It is not a bible, of acoustics or electronics, or indeed of anything else. It aims to clarify the foundations from which good sound can be built.

Section Seven

Further Reading
Useful Addresses
Data Index
A Few Basic Points
Specification
List of drawings
List of photographs
List of tables
Index

Further Reading

Here is a selection of books and periodicals that are available to take the reader further into the subject of theatre sound. The list is not exhaustive but in many cases the books form standard reference works on a particular aspect.

ACOUSTICS

Noise
Rupert Taylor, Pelican

Acoustics, Noise and Buildings
Parkin and Humphreys, Faber

Applied Acoustics
G. Porges, Arnold

Design for Good Acoustics and Noise Control
J. E. Moore, Macmillan

Auditorium Acoustics
Robin Mackenzie, Applied Science

Music, Acoustics and Architecture
Leo Beranek, Wiley

Environmental Acoustics
Leslie L. Doelle, McGraw Hill

VOICE

Voice and Speech in the Theatre
Clifford Turner, Pitman

The Pronunciation of English
Daniel Jones, Cambridge Press

Speech Science
Richard Hoops, Thomas

Speech Training
C. V. Burgess, English University Press

Your Voice and How to Use It
Cicely Berry, Harrap

MICROPHONES

Microphones
A. E. Robertson, Iliffe

Microphones, How They Work and How To Use Them
Martin Clifford, Foulsham

The Use of Microphones
Alec Nisbett, Focal Press

LOUDSPEAKERS
Loudspeakers
G. A. Briggs

ELECTRONIC MUSIC
Electronic Music Production
Alan Douglas, Tab Books
Backstage Rock
Clem Gorman, Pan

RECORDING AND EFFECTS
Tape Recording
Wallace Sharps, Fountain
Noises Off
Frank Napier, Garnet Miller
High Quality Sound Production and Reproduction
Burrell Haddon, Iliffe
Manual of Sound Recording
John Aldred, Fountain
Music in Modern Media
R. E. Dolan, Schirmer

SYSTEM DESIGN
Audio Systems Handbook
Norman Crowhurst, Tab Books
Public Address Handbook
Vivian Capel, Fountain press
Stage Sound
David Collison, Studio Vista
Sound System Engineering
Don and Carolyn Davis, Sams Inc.
Sound in the Theatre
Meyer and Mallory, Audio Library

ELECTRONICS
A Dictionary of Electronics
S. Handel, Penguin
Electronics
Roland Worcester, Hamlyn
Electronics Made Simple
Henry Jacobowitz, W. H. Allen

PERIODICALS

Sightline (May and November)
ABTT, 4 Gt. Pulteney Street, London W1.
Cue (bi-monthl)
Twynam, Kitemore, Faringdon, Oxfordshire.
Entertainment & Arts Management (monthly)
John Offord Pubs. Ltd., PO Box 64, Eastbourne, Sussex.
The Stage (weekly)
The Stage, 47 Bermondsey Street, London SE1.
Theatre Crafts (bi-monthly)
Rodale Press, 33 East Minor Street, Emmaus,
　PA 18048, USA.
Sound and Communications (monthly)
E. G. Rivera Marketing, 7 Mayfield Road, Tunbridge
　Wells, Kent.
Studio Sound (monthly, free to professional engineers
　etc.)
Link House, Dingwall Avenue, Croydon, Surrey.
Tabs (twice yearly)
Rank Strand, PO Box 51, Gt., West Road, Brentford.

Useful Addresses

This is an almost impossible list to compile because
there is no certain way of including everyone, ensuring
that addresses are always up-to-date or of featuring new
companies. Hence we suggest that the two addresses
below will form a good point of contact, especially for
information about consultants, and that these, backed
up by the periodicals listed earlier, will enable the reader
to find his supplier, consultants or whatever . . .

The Association of British Theatre Technicians
(ABTT)
4 Great Pulteney Street, London W1.
Tel: 01-434 3901

The United States Institute of Theatre Technology
(USITT)
1501 Broadway, New York, NY 10036, USA.

Data Sheets

The following data sheets are provided as a quick reference section to the meaning of some of the basic terms used in acoustics and equipment. They are not intended to be a comprehensive glossary, and in each case there is an indication of where, in the book, further reading can be found. The page number indicates the first use of the particular term although it may be used again later. For other references please see the main index.

DATA INDEX

Data Sheet

Sound Theory

Frequency
see page 13

The number of times a sound source vibrates in one second. Measured in Herts, Hz, quantities of 1000 as kHz. High frequencies vibrate many times each second, low frequencies vibrate much less.

Wavelength
see page 12

The distance from a point in a vibration to the same point in another vibration. High frequencies have short wavelengths, low frequences have long wavelengths. The length of waves we can hear range from 1″ to 40′.

Amplitude
see page 14

The strength of the vibration.

Sense of Direction
see page 14

High frequency sounds are more directional than low frequency sounds. The ear can detect horizontal changes of direction better than vertical changes unless given some visual clue.

Speed
see page 14

The speed relates to the air temperature which should always be quoted. At 14°C the speed is 1115′ or about 340m. The speed may be calculated by . . . speed = wavelength × frequency. The speed rises or falls 2′ for each degree centigrade change.

Fundamental Harmonics
see page 16

The initial vibration is the fundamental, harmonics are the subsequent vibrations which are at equal multiples.

Octave
see page 16

Two frequencies, one of which is double the other, are separated by one octave; the two would be said to be in tune.

Transient
see page 17

The way in which a source behaves when first vibrated. The start is the attack, the duration is the sustain and the final is the decay.

Decibel
see page 18

A measure of the difference between two other measurements, one of which may be an agreed international reference point and therefore not stated. Used to compare two sound pressure levels, 2 currents or 2 voltages.

**Sound
Pressure
Levels**
see page 18

The measurement of what sound we hear expressed in decibels by comparison to a zero level, actually the pressure level of a 1000Hz tone. A meter which hears as the human ear does expresses the measurements as dBA, on the 'A' scale.

Data Sheet   Acoustics

Reverberation
see page 30
The way in which a sound bounces around an auditorium after its original source has been cut off. The amount depends on auditorium shape, strength of signal and how much absorption is present.

Reverberation Time
see page 30
The time the sound takes to die away by a defined amount, namely 60dB. There are ideal times for music and speech for a given volume.

Ambiophony Assisted Resonance
see page 32
Two systems of prolonging the reverberation time by electronic means.

Reflection Reflectors
see page 33
The behaviour of sound waves relative to a particular surface. Concave surfaces focus and can lead to echoes, convex surfaces disperse. Concert platforms and modern theatres are provided with reflectors to disperse the sound so that the direct sound waves are enhanced.

Standing Waves Flutter Echoes
see page 38
Standing waves are accentuations of a set of frequencies whose wavelengths are exact multiples of the room's basic dimensions. They are usually harmful. Flutter echoes are caused by parallel walls and prevent sounds from dying away as quickly as might be desirable. Parallel walls can be useful to music. See text.

Grazing Effect
see page 40
The way in which sound is absorbed by the audience, stepping or raking the seating reduces the absorption, and improves sight lines.

Absorption Insulation
see page 42
Absorption relates to the treatment of surfaces so that they may reflect more or less sound. Insulation relates to the way in which a surface may be treated to prevent one sound from passing into another room. The calculation of the amount of absorption is one of the fundamentals of reverberation.

Data Sheet   Microphones

Dynamic
see page 64

Otherwise known as moving coil, signal is induced by action of a moving diahragm and coil upon a magnet.

Condenser
see page 66

.

Signal induced by the interaction of a moving diaphragm and a fixed plate, the two forming a capacitor. These mics are very sensitive and produce the most even response of any kind of mic.

**Polar
Diagram
Pickup**
see page 68

The way in which a mic 'hears' its source, the area in which it is sensitive.

**Cardioid
Hypercardioid**
see page 68

A microphone which is most sensitive in front, generally the one used for stage work.

**Response
Flat**
see page 67

The way in which a microphone de-emphasizes or accentuates particular frequencies. A flat response is an even response and the most desirable.

**Output
Sensitivity**
see page 73

The amount of signal that a mic can generate. Expressed two ways, either in decibels in which case the lower the number the more sensitive the mic. Or in millivolts in which case the higher the value the more sensitive the mic.

**Feedback
Howlround**
see page 68

The high pitched squeal, or ringing caused by sound finding its way out of the loudspeaker back in to the mic and out of the speakers again. It can be lessened by lowering the volume and/or evening out the peaks in the frequency response of the system. Directional mics and speakers are fundamental in helping to overcome this.

Radio Mics
see page 93

Microphones which operate from small transmitters often concealed about the actor or within the mic itself. The result is a wire-free performance. Radio mics are licensed by the Post Office. Their use is not as simple as appears and great care is necessary.

Data Sheet   Mixers

**Input
Channel**
see page 87

That section of a mixer which receives the signal from microphone, tape deck etc.

Modular
see page 86

A mixer which is assembled from a number of plug-in sections. These mixers are usually more versatile and easier to maintain than those constructed from a single fascia.

Mic/Line
see page 87

Input levels for different sources offering two alternative uses for one channel, line level is an agreed international level and one which most professioonal equipment operates at.

**Gain
Sensitivity**
see page 87

The control which regulates the amount of sound the channel is receiving.

Equalisation
see page 87

The area of control over tonal response, mixers may have simple controls over bass and treble or sophisticated control over specific frequencies.

**Auxiliaries
Echo Send
Foldback**
see page 88

A section of the input channel which routes part of the signal to other areas or devices, notably to add echo or to enable musicians to monitor their performance by means of a separate sound system.

**Groups
Subgroups**
see page 93

The section of a mixer where the sound is brought together in combinations, (subgroups) which can then be further combined into stereo (groups).

**Vu
and PPM**
see page 95

The two ways in which the amount of current flowing through the mixer can be displayed on a meter.

**Signal
to Noise
Ratio**
see page 100

The ratio of the signal desired to that of the noise or amount of sound (hiss) generated by the system itself. It is expressed in decibels.

Data Sheet   Other Control Equipment

Equaliser
see page 100

A device which contains filters by which the frequency response of the sound can be changed.

Shelving
see page 101

A filter where the amount of change ceases after a predetermined level.

Bandpass
see page 101

A filter where the response curves towards and then away from the selected frequency.

Parametric
see page 101

A filter that can alter the frequency or rate of attentuation.

Notch
see page 103

A filter that operates a correction at a very specific frequency leaving those around it largely unaffected.

Graphic
see page 102

A filter usually comprised of band-pass filters whos control knobs represent the shape of the resultant sound curve.

Spectrum Analyser
see page 103

A device which displays the sound pressure level of each frequency band enabling filters to be correctly adjusted with ease.

Amplifier
see page 105

The device which accepts the signal from the mixer and gives it the strength to drive the loudspeaker.

RMS
see page 106

The output of the amplifier taken as an average, or root mean square.

Low Impedance 100v Line
see page 106

The way in which the amplifier produces its signal. Constant Voltage, or 100v in the UK, usually associated with public address because of its inferior quality. The alternative is Low Impedance where the speakers must match the amplifier.

Frequency Shefter, Phase Inverter
see page 109

Two devices which are sometimes used to reduce the system's liability to feedback.

Limiter Compressor
see page 109

Two separate devices, often combined which can control the highest and lowest levels of sound volume to defined limits.

**Expander
or Noise
Gate**
see page 110

A device which allows sound to pass only when a predetermined level has been reached.

**Digital
Delay Line**
see page 110

An electronic device which delays the signal to part of the sound system so that it may emerge in sympathy with the live sound.

Data Sheet

Loudspeakers

Moving Coil
see page 114

The loudspeaker which produces sound vibrations by the interaction of a coil acting within a magnet, the coil being connected to the speaker cone.

HF, Tweeter
see page 115

The high frequency unit or driver.

LF, Woofer, Bass Bin
see page 115

The low frequency unit or driver.

Monitor
see page 115

A monitor speaker is a wide range unit of exceptional quality, but it can also be taken to refer to a small relay speaker in control rooms.

Line Source Column
see page 118

A loudspeaker where the cones or drivers are vertically mounted, often the outer cones receive less signal. These units produce even, flat topped wide beams.

Horn Speaker Multicell
see page 121

A speaker which contains a metal cone attached to the coil. It is more efficient than the moving coil speaker and deals with the middle and upper frequencies.

Wedge
see page 117

A special wedge shaped speaker for stage working in the foldback system.

Stack
see page 119

A vertical assembly of loudspeakers, usually of the bass bin variety and associated with the pop industry.

Data Sheet   Statistics

**Sound
Pressure
Level**
see page 24   Relative to zero level, 1000Hz tone, 0dB.

**Electrical
Power
Level**
see page 95   Relative to 0.001 watt or 0.775 volts across 600 ohm.

Human Voice Fundamentals see page 20		
Bass		85-340 Hz
Baritone		90-380 Hz
Tenor		125-460 Hz
Alto		130-680 Hz
Contralto		180-600 Hz
Soprano		225-1000 Hz
Male Speech		125 Hz
Female Speech		210 Hz
Trained Male Speech		140 Hz
Trained Female Speech		230 Hz
Fundamentals		125-250 Hz
Vowels		350-2000 Hz
Consonants		1500-4000 Hz

**Human Voice
Power**
see page 21

62.5-500 Hz	60% of power of voice, 5% intelligibility
500-1000 Hz	35% of power, 35% intelligibility
1000-8000 Hz	5% of power, 60% intelligibility

Whisper	30 dBA
Conversation	50 dBA
Lecturer	60 dBA
Actor	70 dBA

(all measured at 10' (3m)).

**Human
Ear**
see page 24

Best range when young, pure tones, 16Hz—20kHz
Most sensitive, 3 kHz—5 kHz range.
Minimum change in intensity detectable under ideal conditions, 1 dB, normally about 2 dB.

High Sound Level Exposure
see page 25

Tables of Exposure to Industrial Noise

UK

90 dBA	8 hr. per day max.
93 dBA	4 hr. per day max.
96 dBA	2 hr. per day max.
99 dBA	1 hr. per day max.
102 dBA	½ hr. per day max.
105 dBA	¼ hr. per day max.

USA (OSHA)

90 dBA	8 hr. per day max.
95 dBA	4 hr. per day max.
100 dBA	2 hr. per day max.
105 dBA	1 hr. per day max.
110 dBA	½ hr. per day max.
115 dBA	¼ hr. per day max.

Reverberation Times
see page 30

Measured at full capacity and in the 500 Hz - 100 Hz band.

Covent Garden Opera House	1.2
Free Trade Hall Manchester	1.6
Royal Festival Hall	1.6
Royal Albert Hall	2.9
Teatro La Scala Milan	1.2

Ideal Volumes and Areas
see page 31

Max per seat for speech from 2.3 cu. m to 4.3 cu. m (80 to 150 cu. ft.), best option per seat for speech 3.1 cu. m. (110 cu. ft.), max per seat for music from 4.5 cu. m. to 7.4. cu. m. (160 to 260 cu. ft.), best option for music 5.7 cu. m. (200 cu. ft.), max for pit musician in area 1.0 sq. m. to 1.5 sq .m..

Sabine Formula for RT
see page 43

Reverberation Time =

$$\frac{0.16 \text{ (metric constant)} \times \text{volume in metres}}{\text{total absorption in sabin metric units}}$$

The imperial formula is . . .

Reverberation Time =

$$\frac{0.05 \times \text{volume in cubic feet}}{\text{total absorption in square feet sabin units}}$$

Sample Absorption Coefficients
see page 43

	250 Hz	500 Hz	1000 Hz
Brick	0.04	0.02	0.04
Concrete	0.02	0.02	0.04

	250 Hz	500 Hz	1000 Hz
Plaster, solid	0.03	0.02	0.03
Thick carpet	0.25	0.5	0.5
Air/cu. m.	nil	nil	0.003
Audience in Upholstered seat	0.4	0.46	0.46
Empty wood seat	nil	0.15	nil
Rostrum/sq. m.	0.1	nil	nil

Reduction Indices of Walls Etc.
see page 49

4″ (100 mm) brick plastered both sides	40 dB
9″ (230 mm) brick plastered both sides	52 dB
4″ brick walls, 2″ (50 mm) cavity and both sides plastered	56 dB
6″ concrete block, solid and plastered	50 dB
3/8″ (10 mm) gypsum wall board	26 dB
1/2″ (13 mm) gypsum wall board	28 dB
5/8″ (16 mm) gypsum wall board	31 dB
Partition of 3/8″ plastered gypsum with 4″ cavity	43 dB

Specifications

Mixer
see page 87

Input to match 200 ohm mic, balanced.
System gain—30 to 80 dB in 10 dB steps, line input 100k ohm.
Sensitivity—70 to + 10 dB in 10 dB steps.
Frequency controls, 100 Hz and 10 kHz + 16 dB.

Signal to noise ratio, better than 100 dB.
Response flat over 20-20 kHz.

Typical filter points
40, 50, 63, 100, 125, 160, 200, 250, 315, 400, 500, 630, 800, 1000, 1250, 1600, 2500, 3150, 4000, 5000, 6300, 8000, 10000, 12500, 16000 Hz.

Amplifier, Typical
see page 105

Total harmonic distortion less than 0.02% rated output at a frequency of 1 kHz less than 0.03% at rated output 30 Hz—20 kHz. Response ± 3 dB over 20 Hz—20 kHz. Noise better than 80 dB. 200 watt rms into 8 ohms, 100 watts rms into 16 ohms.

Speakers
Typical
see page 114

3 way system response 50 Hz—19 kHz, 118 dB SPL at 10' from 50 w. Line source response, 65 Hz—18 kHz + 3 dB, 112 dB SPL at 10' from full power. Horn response, 170 Hz—13 kHz + 3 dB, 120 dB SPL at 10' from full power.

Time Delay
Calculations
see page 110

Time delay is required if the direct and amplified sound paths to a point, (or two amplified paths to a point), differ by a time of more than 40ms. This represents about 40' at a temperature of 14°C. The Hass effect (see text) denotes levels relative to maintaining the direction effect of the source.

Decibels
see page 136

Adding two sound pressure levels that are the same, add 3 dB, that is two levels of say 60 dB will give a level of 63 dB adding two that are not the same.

Difference in Signals	Add to Larger Signal
1dB	2.5dB
2	2.1
3	1.7
4	1.4
5	1.1
6	.97
7	.79
8	.63
9	.51
10	.43
11	.35
12	.26

Distance
see page 22

Each time the distance from the sound source is doubled the sound pressure level falls by 6 dB. This does not take into account the contribution from the acoustic which would prevent any loss at some distance from the source where reverberation would take over.

Power
see page

Each time the power to a loudspeaker is halved the level of intensity falls by 3 dB and the SPL falls by 6 dB (and vice versa if the power is doubled).

Number of
Mics Live
see page 78

Each time the number of live microphones is doubled the sound level is effectively reduced by 3 dB otherwise feedback would result.

Cable Guide
see page 158

8 ohm 50m up to 100w	0.75 sq. mm.
8 ohm 50m 100w to 400w	2.5 sq. mm.
8 ohm 50m 400w to 1000w	4.0 sq. mm.
100 v line up to 100w	0.5 sq. mm.
100 v line 100w to 1000w	1.0 sq. mm.

**Plug and
Socket Guide**
see page 158

Mic level carriers are male, even numbers (xir - 3 - 12c). Speaker level carriers are usually female, odd numbers (xir - 4 - 11c).

Mic carriers are three pin, speakers three or four pin. (See text)

'A Few Basic Points'

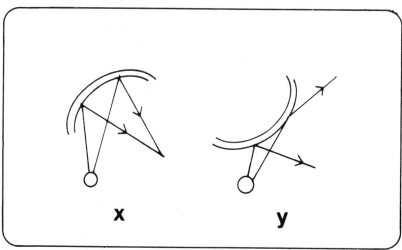

Concave surfaces (x) like domes and cornices can focus the sound and create echoes, convex surfaces (y) will disperse the sound and thus are often found in reflectors over stages and orchestras. (see page 33)

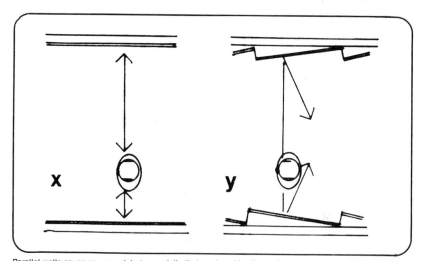

Parallel walls cause any sound, but especially that produced by the audience, to continue bouncing across the auditorium as in (x). In (y) the walls have been angled slightly so that the sound will be dispersed. This will help the show sound also. It should be noted that parallel walls have some advantages in musical events. (see page 38).

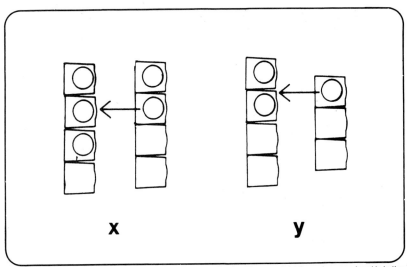

Seating arranged in neat rows one behind the other can often lead to poor sight lines since one head is in line with another, (x). If the seats are staggered as in (y) then one head looks between the heads of those in front. This helps sound as well as sight, (see page 40).

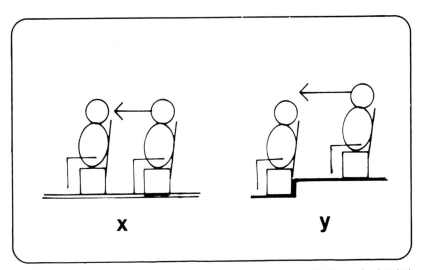

A similar situation occurs on level floors as in (x), if the floor is stepped or sloped (y) then one head can look over the row in front. Again this helps sound as well as sight. In multipurpose auditoria where flat floors are popular, it is helpful to provide some tiering for the rear rows. A combination of stepping and staggering is particularly effective.

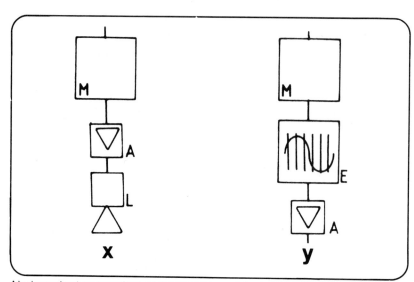

A basic sound system passes the signal from mixer M to amp A then to speaker L, as in (x), in (y) an extra unit, the graphic equaliser E, is introduced to fine tune the system to the particular acoustics of the theatre. The resultant sound could be cleaner, flatter and less likely to feed back than in (x). (see page 101)

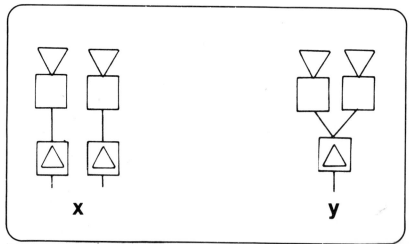

In (x) one amplifier is serving two speakers, they are both obliged to compromise on an ideal level and if the amp failed, both would die. In (y) each speaker is provided with its own amp, this enables more precise balances to take place and, in the event of failure, would still leave one speaker producing sound. (see page 144).

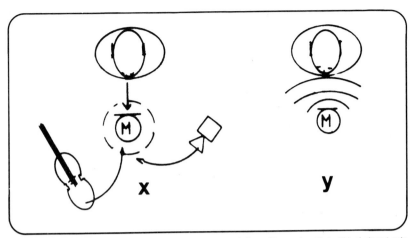

If microphones (m) are omnidirectional they will pick up sounds from all around so that will include not only the performer but also audience and instruments nearby, and sound from the loudspeaker which could cause feedback (x). A unidirectional mic in (y), sometimes called cardioid, will hear only the performer unless it is turned up to a very high level in which case it, too, will hear other sources although to a lesser extent than in (x) (see page 68).

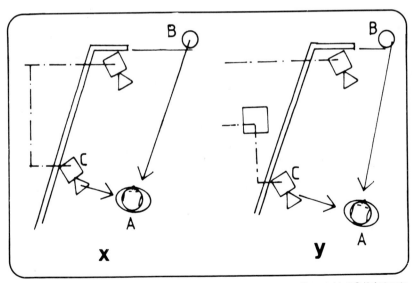

In large auditoria a second set of speakers is often provided to serve seats near the rear, (x), at C. Unfortunately they are usually connected to the main speakers on the pros arch so that the sound CA reaches the audience before the live sound BA, this destroys the directional effect. The answer is to provide an electronic delay into the line feeding C, in fact so that the live sound BA reaches the audience just before the delayed sound CA, the directional effect is preserved even though the amplified sound CA might be louder than the live sound BA. (see page 110).

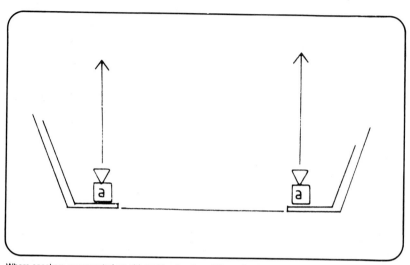

Where speakers are mounted on either side of a stage, it is a mistake to fix them so that their beams pass straight down the theatre parallel to the centre line. The audience tends to look towards the centre of the stage and this positioning means that the sound is loudest at the ear further away from the stage which is not authentic.

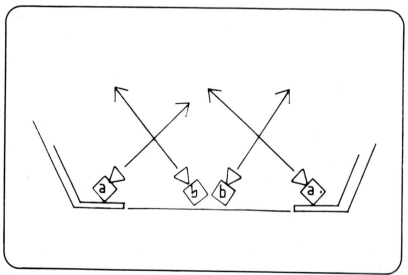

The answer is to angle the beams from the loudspeakers (a) so that they cross towards the centre, the sound now comes from the stage. This can lead to feedback because the side beam of the speaker is closer to the stage mics, so the actual positioning must be by trial and error if feedback cannot be eliminated by other methods. The best speaker position however is centrally over the pros arch or stage at (b). (see page 131).

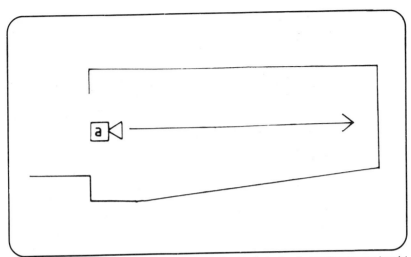

The speaker should not be fixed so that its beam passes level to the back wall where it may cause harmful reflections. In this position the highly directional upper frequencies, where most of the clarity lies, pass over the heads of the audience.

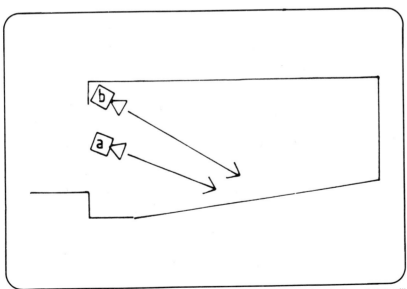

The answer is to angle the unit down into the stalls. This has to be carefully done otherwise the rear seats will lose the beam (a). Again a position over the arch is preferable at (b). (see page 131).

Sound System Specification

The following specification is a copy of that drawn up by a consultant for a London Theatre and the system it describes is now installed and working. The specification aims to help those quoting by means of a schematic diagram (site plans were also available) and by means of a description how each item in the system was to be used. The client and his consultant had very clear ideas all through as to what was required, thus where both liked a particular product, the manufacturer is named. Elsewhere the specification is based on a particular piece of equipment, but this is not named in order that manufacturers can feel free to offer their own version of what is required.

Since all companies quoting were known to both consultant and client, it was not necessary to build into the spec. requests for track record (turnover, profit after tax, number of employees, references etc.) but this might be useful where committee decisions are involved and none of the companies are known.

The · · · Theatre Sound Specification

Contents

1.1 Requirement

This specification covers the provision, with installation and commissioning, of a new sound system to be installed at the theatre. The contractor is required to provide detailed specifications with itemised costings of that which he considers will meet the requirements of this document. The price should include the spares, commissioning and generally leaving the system in working order. The cost should take into account attendance and working with the company who will be responsible for any actual electrical or sound installation work involved. They are to be instructed by the approved contractor, in association with the consultants of the appropriate requirements.

1.2 Variations

Contractors are permitted to offer variations to this document, but only where detailed explanation is given will the variation be considered.

1.3 Site Visit

Any contractor who wishes to visit the site may do so but only by contacting the consultant first. Direct contact with the client on site is not permitted.

1.4 Safety

It should be borne in mind that the ultimate client will be the Greater London Council and therefore the equipment proposed should match the kind of safety standards normally imposed by that organisation. It is possible that some items require to be approved by the GLC and therefore no item that carries main current should be custom built but should be standard item, compatible with appropriate British Standards. Please note that the building is used for practical education in the theatre arts. The equipment should therefore withstand a certain amount of structural and operational misuse without impairing safety.

1.5 Brief

Please note that this document is the result of agreement on the brief given to the consultant by the actual existing operators of the current sound installation.

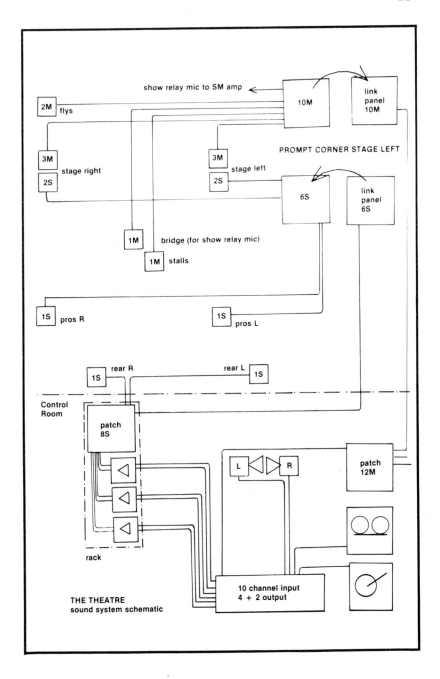

show relay mic to SM amp

2M | flys

10M

link panel 10M

PROMPT CORNER STAGE LEFT

3M | stage right

3M | stage left

2S

2S

6S

link panel 6S

1M | bridge (for show relay mic)

1M | stalls

1S | pros R

1S | pros L

rear R

1S

rear L | 1S

Control Room

patch 8S

L ▷◁ R

patch 12M

rack

THE THEATRE
sound system schematic

10 channel input
4 + 2 output

Section Three · The Mixer

3.1 Requirement

Since the unit may be envisaged as being installed for a number of years, it is vital that not only does it encompass today's requirements but also provides scope for those of tomorrow as its users become more familiar with its capabilities. In this respect stereo mixing is vital today but it is necessary to be able to provide four outputs for simultaneous stereo mic balancing overlayed with twin channel sound effects. At the same time at least two auxiliary mixes are required for echo and foldback. The desk should be of table top variety since it will be moved backstage on occasions. It is likely that children will operate it on occasion and therefore all but the gain control must be capable of being covered by means of transparent covers. Notwithstanding this all controls must be coloured to distinguish one section from the next and the calibrations must be clearly visible to an operator seated and in dim lighting. It would be an advantage to be able to re-position the input and output modules as desired. Only modular systems will be considered.

3.2 Item

There shall be 10 input channels accepting microphone level signals from 200 ohm balanced microphones and this input shall be provided with a sensitivity control providing up to 65dB of gain; line level signals shall also be available as an alternative input by means of a signal switch; there shall be separate boost or cut controls for both high and low frequencies plus or minus 16dB, the ability to select the shelving frequency would be an advantage; there shall also be apparametric mid range sweep control with 16dB boost or cut over 300Hz to 10kHz; an equalisation cut switch shall also be provided; there shall be a minimum of two auxiliary sends with rotary gain control selectable to either pre or post fader; the channel output shall be selectable to four groups simultaneously, alternatively two sub groups and two main outputs will be acceptable; the selection shall be by internally illuminated switches or preferably those of the Schadow variety and the pan control shall affect the odd and even numbered groups; the channel shall also be provided with an 'on' push self illuminating, a prefade listen push self illuminating, and an illuminated Vu meter; a conductive plastic track fader shall be provided with write on strip.

The unweighted noise level for 200 ohm source shall be better than —120dBm, maximum output shall be + 20dBm with distortion at 1kHz better than 0.05% THD, the frequency response shall be plus or minus 1dB over 20Hz-20kHz.

The system shall provide four main outputs and it will be acceptable if these are acheived with the aid of group sub master modules. Each output is to be provided with an illuminated meter. LED PPM's are preferable but not essential, moving coil Vu's will be acceptable. Each group should also have the following facilities, self illuminating prefade listen push, self illuminating channel on push, auxillary return gain (for echo), auxilliary input gain (for submix etc.), monitor level, conductuve plastic track fader.

It is required to be able to monitor the auxiliary mixes individually, the prefade chain, the individual group outputs, and the overall mix. Gain controls should be provided for auxiliary outputs and for the prefade chain.

It is not a requirement but it would be an advantage to have internally mounted microphone with talkback to output groups and auxiliaries. Similarly an oscillator would be an advantage.

Overall performance shall be; maximum mic gain 70dB, maximum line gain 10dB; maximum output level into 5k ohm and above + 20dBm, + 15dBm into 600 ohm; the frequency response from line input to group output shall be plus or minus 1dB over 20Hz to 20kHz; the distortion shall be better than 0.05%, THD measured also line input to group output; the noise level (unweighted) shall be—70dBm with all channels working to one group.

All inputs and outputs shall be either at the rear or top mounted in which case they shall be concealed. The mic inputs shall be XLR-3-31. Line inputs may be identical but preferably via jack socket. Outputs shall be via XLR-3-32 and each shall be provided additionally with a lead to connect to power amplifiers. These to be provided at the commissioning stage.

3.3 Accesories

As previously mentioned the mixer requires transparent covers to prevent less experienced hands from adjusting the controls. In addition the unit should be provided with suitable spare fuses and lamps etc. and **no** system will be considered without **prior** knowledge of the handbook.

3.4 Pricing

The pricing shall be for a complete wired and tested unit.

Section Four · Amplification

4.1 Requirement

In all the mixer provides six outputs which may be a combination of mic mixes with effects overlay or multichannel effects or multichannel mic with foldback. Each output requires its own amplifier. Since the prime useage of the system would require four amplifiers only, numbers five and six may be considered for auxiliary and spare functions. The amplifiers need mounting in as compact a way as possible with foolproof changeover in the event of failure and adjacent to the speaker patch panel.

4.2 Item

The amplifiers shall be mounted in a metal equipment rack which shall also contain the speaker patch panel mounted at the top of the unit. The rack shall have a side access panel so that maintenance is possible with the unit positioned against a wall. All controls including the patch panel shall be mounted on the fascia which shall be protected by a transparent lockable door.

Each amplifier shall produce at least 200w rms into 8 ohms and at least 300w rms into 4 ohms at the clip point. The harmonic distortion at all levels up to the clip point shall be less than 0.02%. The frequency response shall be plus or minus 1dB 10Hz-20kHz. The noise level shall be 105dB below 180w into 8 ohms over 10Hz to 20kHz.

Each unit shall be provided with a force cooling dissipator drawing the air through the front panel. This action shall not be impeded by the transparent rack door. The dissipator shall be provided with one thermal switch which activates the fan when the dissipator temperature reaches approximately 63°C.

The second switch shall turn the mains power to the amplifier off in the event of the output stage reaching a temperature of 90°C. The unit shall additionally be provided with short circuit, mismatch and open circuit protection. For easy maintenance all driver circuits and output devices shall be mounted on a single module with easily released connector. The unit shall have a gain control mounted on the fascia. All inputs and outputs shall be at the rear.

The six amplifier outputs shall be brought out to the patch panel terminating in XLR-4-31. Six jump leads shall then be provided (XLR-4-12c to XLR-4-11c) to present the signal to the loudspeaker connections of which there shall be 8 in XLR-4-32. The low impedance being connected to pins 1 and 2.

4.3 Pricing

The whole unit shall be priced as a wired and tested unit but individual costs for each amplifier shall also be shown.

Section Five · Microphones

5.1 Requirement

The theatre is already in possession of units which are suitable for recording or reinforcement work over a wide range. There is a need for units for voice reinforcement and they should take into account the wide dynamic range of the system and therefore provide a high gain before feedback. The units should be provided with a pop gag and have sufficient guarantee to take into account the occasional rough handling likely with children.

5.2 Item

The unit provided shall be Electrovoice DS35 professional dynamic cardioid microphone having a response of 60 Hz—17,000 Hz, 150 ohm impedance, output—60 dB, Switchcraft A3F connector and 15′ cable.

5.3 Accesories

The above unit shall be provided with a 312A clamp fitted with suitable thread adaptor for both AKG telescopic floor stand ref ST200 and Electrovoice low profile desk stand ref 422. Each unit shall additionally be supplied with an extension cable 25' long fitted with Cannon or matching connectors ultimately terminating in XLR-3-12c or equivalent. All the above named items shall be provided.

5.4 Pricing

Each item shall be separately priced, the microphone shall have unconditional professional warranty.

Section Six · Loudspeakers

6.1 Requirement

For the most part the theatre requires units through which to replay taped music or sound effects. However microphone useage is growing especially with productions hiring the theatre. The wide dynamic range of the units should not be provided without taking microphone working into account and the flatter response achieved from the units the better since no equalisers are available outside of those on the main channels on the desk. Units are to be positioned either side of the proscenium arch serving the single tier 394 seats (see site drawings). Other units are to be provided as portable effects/music/foldback monitors.

6.2 Item

Each unit shall have a frequency response of at least 75Hz—16kHz through a minimum of two loudspeaker inserts and shall produce a sound pressure level measured at 100w 4' of 115dB. The power rating of the unit shall be 100w at 8 ohm. Auditorium units shall be finished to match the decor, this to be by discussion with the approved contractor and backstage units shall be in black with metal edging strips and castored bases. Each speaker shall be fitted with a Cannon connector ref XLR-4-12c wherein two pins only are used for low impedance.

6.3 Accesories

The auditorium units shall be mounted from a vertical boom positioned at the side of the proscenium arch.

The contractor should provide a provisional sum, subject to a site survey, for two such units in alloy 15' long with ceiling plate and 18" wall bracket mounted each four adjustable speaker brackets.

6.4 Pricing

It is considered that the auditorium is wide enough to jusitfy four auditorium units whilst two units are requried on stage. Each item is to be separately priced.

Section Seven · Outlet Panels

7.1 Requirements

To replace and supplement the existing outlet panels with professional standard hard wearing connectors. The final details will be subject to site survey in association with the electrical contractor.

7.2 Items

In all cases the pricing should include the rear mounting box which will be supplied to the electrical contractor, in addition to the actual socket plate.
Finishes will be engraved satin chrome throughout. The following are required:

1 off 2 mic socket for flys
2 off 3 mic socket for stage dips
2 off 1 mic socket for bridge and stalls
The above being XLR-3-31

2 off 2 speaker sockets for dips
4 off 1 speaker socket for auditorium
The above being XLR-4-31

1 off mic termination panel for stage, 10 way, XLR-3-32
1 off mic link panel to control room, 10 way, XLR-3-31

10 jump leads for above, XLR-3-11c to XLR-3-12c

1 off speaker termination panel for stage, 6 way, XLR-4-32

1 off speaker link panel to control room, 6 way, XLR-4-31

6 jump leads for above XLR-4-11c to XLR-4-12c

1 patch panel for control room mic terminations, 12 way XLR-3-32

12 jump leads from above to mixing desk, 6' long terminating XLR-3-11c to XLR-3-12c

7.3 Pricing

Prices are required for each individual panel or socket outlet, and totals for each collection of jump leads.

Section Eight-Ancillary Items

8.1 Disc Unit

Supply one transcription turntable in lockable desk top box. The unit is to operate at 33⅓ rpm and 45 rpm and it would be an advantage if the speed was variable between the two. The lowering arm is to be provided with a cueing device. The stereo cartridge is to be provided with a sturdy stylus. Line output preamplifier with 6' lead and jack plug termination is also required.

8.2 Tape Unit

Supply one Sonifex GFX 500 cartridge machine with NAB equalisation and 6' lead with jack plug termination.

8.3 Reverb Unit

Supply one freestanding unit to add mono reverberation to occasional special mic and taped effects. The unit should be comparable to the old Grampian reverb unit.

8.4 Monitors

Two good quality monitor loudspeakers should be provided for the control room. You may advise accordingly but please note that the room is not accessible to the theatre acoustic and is also used for recording. The Monitors should be small. Also provide one good quality headset.

8.5 Stage Manager

Provide one wall mounting amplification unit with mixer having bass and treble boost and cut controls and separate inputs with volume controls for the show relay mic and overriding stage managers mic.

Provide on the stage manager's desk (existing), one gooseneck mic with press to talk push and one hand wander mic with press to talk push which, when used, mutes the gooseneck mic. Also provide, for inclusion into the SM desk, one switch panel which limits the SM calls to the two control room speakers only. The other selector limits the calls to dressing rooms.

Provide a per unit cost, of dressing room speakers with volume operative on show relay alone. Also provide one show relay mic, D190 or equivalent with 15' lead, hook clamp and XLR-3-12c.

It may be discussed at a later date whether the show relay cum SM paging is a selectable/overriding feature of the control room monitors. It may be that the desk itself could take care of this feature since ideally both programme and paging should not interfere.

8.6 Pricing

As indicated on a per unit cost basis for each separate item.

Section Nine - Installation and Commissioning

9.1 Installation

A certain amount of sound wiring is already in use for the current system but will need extending for the system proposed. This work will be undertaken by a commercial company who will work to specifications provided by the approved contractor in discussion with the consultant. You are advised that a detailed site survey will be necessary at that stage in order to avoid numerous runs of thyristor lighting wiring. The specification to the supplier should include for any builder's work to form part of their contract by discussion with the consultant. The actual scope of this document covers supply and commissioning.

9.2 Commissioning

Indicate the daily rate per engineer of the cost of commissioning and estimate the likely total based on unimpeded working time from correctly installed cabling.

9.3 Maintenance

Notwithstanding the provisions of the Sale of Goods and Implied terms Act, all items should be provided with instructions on first line maintenance by the theatre staff, backed up with suitable fuses etc. However please indicate the likely cost of two service visits per annum, independant of actual replacement parts outside the first year.

List of Drawings

List of Photographs

Section 5

Section 6

List of Tables

Index